VICTORIAN WADHURST
GLIMPSES OF OUR PAST

AN OCCASIONAL PUBLICATION

BY THE WADHURST HISTORY SOCIETY

DECEMBER 2005

TABLE OF CONTENTS

© 2005 for the Wadhurst History Society

ISBN 0-9545802-1-4

Foreword

Michael Harte

The Wadhurst History Society was founded at the end of 2003, as a follow-up to the celebrations of the 750th anniversary of the granting of a charter to Archbishop Boniface by King Henry III for 'a Market at Wadhurst in the County of Sussex on the Saturday of each week and ..... a Fair every year to last for three days namely on the Vigil, the Day & the Morrow of the Feast of the Apostles Peter & Paul.'

Apart from offering its members monthly talks on a local history theme, and outings and social functions, the Society has also set up a series of working groups to explore our own history:

Development of Wadhurst
Industry and agriculture
Family history
Estates and buildings
Oral history

To provide a focus for the first two years' work, the groups have concentrated on the Victorian period: for the oral history group this has not been of particular relevance as few of the older inhabitants have direct recollections of that era - instead that group has concentrated on interviewing as many long-time residents as possible. Their work will feature in a subsequent occasional publication from the Society.

The other groups have inevitably been selective in the areas they have studied - first because of limits on the time that individuals can make available - not all are retired; secondly because, even with a limit to the Victorian era, the amount of material that could be investigated is very large.

Working methods have varied from extensive reading of existing literature, through research in the East Sussex Record Office in Lewes, in the College of Arms and in the National Archives in Kew, to discussions with experts in the locality. The research groups contain few expert historians but have made up for any lack of specialist expertise with an abundance of enthusiasm.

Whilst the articles which follow have all been attributed to a single author, there have been many others involved in the work and much of the research has been collective and benefited from group discussion. As overall editor, I have sought to maintain a degree of consistency in the articles but have not felt it appropriate to exercise the degree of editorial control that others with a more professional background might have done; we hope, however, that all the articles will be of interest and will extend the reader's knowledge of Victorian Wadhurst. Some articles go further and reveal new information about our past - or present existing information in a more coherent form.

Our working methods have meant that we have drawn on existing published material for background; at the end of most articles is a list of the key sources consulted. We have made efforts to seek agreement to the direct use of published material wherever possible - not always with success. The key sources have been:

Kenneth F. Ascott: *The Education of Wadhurst*, The Book Guild, 1998

Stan Cosham & Michael Harte: *Wadhurst Then and Now*, Greenman Enterprise 2003

Mrs Rhys Davids [updated by Alfred Wace]: *The Story of Wadhurst*, Courier Printing & Publishing 1923

Brian Harwood: *The High Weald in Old Photographs*, Alan Sutton Publishing 1990

The High Weald - a Second Selection, Alan Sutton Publishing 1993

Alan Savidge and Oliver Mason: *Wadhurst - Town of the High Weald* Meresborough Books 1998

The archives at the East Sussex Record Office [ESRO] in Lewes have proved of invaluable help and our thanks are due to all the staff, whose professional and knowledgeable assistance has made our task so much easier.

Thanks are also due to those who have transcribed census returns for the period 1841 - 1901, Julian Groves [via the Tunbridge Wells Family History Society] for 1841, 1861 and 1891; June Barnes for 1851; and the Mormon Church for 1881. 1871 was transcribed by me, from microfilm on CD produced by S&N British Data Archive; 1901 comes from the on-line version available through www.ancestry.co.uk.

Part of the Wadhurst tithe map of 1840 [IR 30/35/274] has been used in several articles, with permission of the National Archive. Brian Harwood's books have been invaluable for our study of the workhouse. We also referred on many occasions to the map of central Wadhurst, drawn by William Courthope in the 1850s and now in the College of Arms.

Many of the illustrations are taken from the Bocking Collection: we are grateful to the Wadhurst Parish Council and the Bocking trustees for permission to use them; Jennet Hemsley was most helpful in finding the originals for scanning. Tony Trevaskes of the Wadhurst Post Office kindly allowed us to use postcards in his own collection.

Finally a note for younger readers: rather than translate pre-decimal currency every time it is mentioned in the text, the following note may help. The pound used to be divided into twenty shillings, each equivalent to 5 new pence; in turn the shilling was divided into 12 old pennies, each equivalent to 5/12 of a new penny– to put it another way one new penny is worth 2.4 old pennies. The old style currency was written £1 / 2 /6, £1.2s.6d. or £1 - 2 - 6 and spoken 'one pound two shillings and sixpence', equivalent to £1.125 today. We have not attempted to put a value in purchasing power to the Victorian pound against today's money.

WADHURST SEEN THROUGH THE VICTORIAN
CENSUS RETURNS
MICHAEL HARTE

A count has been made of the population in England and Wales from the beginning of the 19th century but until 1841 no detail was recorded at the individual level. The enumerators for the 1841 census were required to collect the names of each individual living in every household, together with age [recorded in bands] and occupation; an indication of county of birth was usually entered but, for local research purposes, the critical data - full address - were not recorded. In 1851, the head of household was entered, as was the individual's relation to the head; marital status and place of birth was also recorded and somewhat more detail provided of addresses. The returns for 1851 are not, however, sufficient to give certainty of location across the whole parish: for example, 11 households are listed under the address 'Lower Turnpike Gate' - essentially the 5 properties now known as Laurel Bank.

For the 1861 census, the same details were collected but the address information is less precise: there are no entries for 'Lower Turnpike Gate' - all are shown as 'Village'. In 1871, there is a similar lack of detail; in 1881 the address details usually make it possible to identify the precise property in the listing but imprecision creeps in again for 1891 and 1901 when most of the centre of Wadhurst is simply described as 'Town'.

Enumerators were required to go round the parish and record in their own hand the details of all those in each household resident on census night; these records were then checked by a registrar and signed off by the superintendent registrar for the area; the original records are now available on microfiche. For the Wadhurst parish, all the microfiche records have been transcribed to provide computer searchable data; various individuals - listed in the foreword - have carried out this tedious task; but without it, compiling lists and analysing details would be almost impossible.

For census purposes, Wadhurst parish was divided into districts: the definition of their boundaries remain essentially constant over the whole period from 1851 to 1901. The census does not use the traditional Wadhurst division into quarters: Town, Bibleham, Riseden, Faircrouch, Week and Cousley Wood as identified by Alfred Wace.

The census districts, precisely as described for the 1871 returns, are:

"1   Village District, comprises so much of the Parish as lies between the sixth mile stone, on the Tunbridge Wells Road, and the Lower Toll Gate House, on both sides of the Road, as is encompassed by a line, including Lower Prospect House, Lower Tollgate etc

2   Cockmount District, comprises all that part of the Parish on the North side of the Turnpike Road from near where the Toll Gate formerly stood to Riverhall Brook, then on the East side of the Brook to Sewers Bridge, the West of the Road to Brooklands, then South of the Road to Pitt House, and Sparrows Green, and near where the Toll Gate formerly stood; including Great Durgates, Railway Tavern, Dewhurst, Swatlands, Brookland Cottage, a Cottage near Bones', Three Oaks, Lambskin Corner, Stonebridge, Cockmount, and part of Sparrows Green etc etc

3   Great Shoesmiths District, comprises all that part of the Parish lying on the North and East side of the Road from Pitt House to Sewers Bridge, then on the South of the stream to Bartley Mill, then on the West of the Road to Pitt House; including Whitegates, Moons, Newlands Fields, Great Shoesmiths, Bartley Cottages, Stivers, Great Buckland Hill, Weel & Farm [? *Wick Farm*], Perrins, Woods Green, Turners Green, etc etc

4   Pitt House District, comprises all that part of the Parish on the East side of the Road from Pitt House, to Little Buckland Hill, then on the North side of the Road to Bartley Mill, then South of the Parish Boundary, to Slade Green, on the Wadhurst and Lamberhurst Turnpike Road and West of the Road to Pitt House, including Horsegrove, Gate House, Wickhurst, Busses Green, White Magpie House near Slade Gate, part of Cousleywood, Pell Green, Pitt House etc etc

5   Great Pell District, comprises all that part of the Parish on the East side of the Wadhurst and Lamberhurst Turnpike Road, from Sparrows Green to Slade Gate, then on the South and East side of the Parish Boundary to Shovers Green, then on the North side of the Tunbridge Wells Turnpike Road to the Wadhurst Lower Turnpike Gate and Villiage [*sic*] Boundary to Sparrows Green, including part of Cousley Wood, Sparrowsgreen, Newhouse, Great Pell, Sodom, Ladysmeads, Markwicks, Little Butts, Great Pell Cottage, Foxhole, Moseham, Little Pell, Vicarage Green etc etc.

6   Shovers Green District, comprises all that Part of the Parish on the South of the Tunbridge Wells Turnpike Road and Village Boundary from Durgates to Shovers Green then on the West of the Parish Boundary to the Boundary of the Tidebrook Ecclesiastical District then on the South and East of that District to Best Beech Hill Road to Durgates including the Castle and Castle Lodge Foxes Stone Cross Shovers Green Church Settle and Cottage near the Railway Crouches Mill Land Buttons Scrag Oak Beer House Snape Wood Cottages Smith's near Best Beech Hill South Park etc etc

7   Faircrouch District, comprises all that part of the Parish on the West side of the Road from Little Durgates to the Boundary of the Tidebrook Ecclesiastical District at Bestbeachill [*sic*] then on the North of the Boundary of that District to Markcross then East of the Parish Boundary to Riverhall Mill and South of the Tunbridge-Wells Turnpike Road to Little Durgates including

Tapsells, Faircrouch Styles Cottage Westons Frankham Farm at [*sic*] Cottages at Back, Partridges Early Buckhurst Ivy Chimney Railway Station Little Durgates etc etc

8   Tidebrook Ecclesiastical District - East Part, comprises all that part of the Parish lying East of the Road from Tidebrook river, on the Wadhurst and Mayfield Road, to the Windmill, and from a line marked by stones through Snape Farm to Snape Wood Stream, and following the stream on the South side of the boundary of the Parish - again, near the Tidebrook River then on the North side of the river as a boundary of the Parish to the Wadhurst and Mayfield Road ....[*text erased*].... Reed Farm, Windmill, Snape Farm, Wenbon's, Flattinden, Dens, Coomb Farm etc etc

9   Tidebrook Ecclestiastical District (West part), comprises all that part of the Parish of Wadhurst, lying West of the Road from Tidebrook River on the Wadhurst and Mayfield road to Bestbeech Hill, then on the South of the Markcross road including One Hundred yards on the North side of the said road as marked out on the Plan by a red line up to Markcross then on the North East side of the Parish Boundary to the Wadhurst and Mayfield road at the Tidebrook River, including Towngate, Newhouse, Bestbeech Hill, Skinners, Beggars Bush, Frankham House, Markcross House, Earls, Bassetts, Pennybridge etc etc."

For each census, summary sheets were produced, listing the number of people - split between male and female, the number of schedules [essentially individual buildings] and households [often more than one to a schedule], and the number of empty properties. The enumerators were local men, usually of some standing - and of course able to write. For our returns, reading the handwriting is generally not a problem. For 1871 the Wadhurst enumerators were:

-1- James Cheesman - corn merchant
-2- Jabez Smith - postmaster
-3- Rowland Smith - butcher master
-4- Jacob Pitt - inn keeper of The Greyhound
-5- Charles Brissenden - farmer of 200 acres
-6- Henry Smith - currier
-7- Henry George Wallis - bricklayer master employing 4 men
-8- Dennis Tompsett - farmer of 128 acres
-9- Richard Henry White - timekeeper on buildings

Notes were also made of the number of visitors to the district and of those who were idiots, deaf and dumb or blind.

Over the 7 censuses, there are 20800 individual entries; analysis has therefore required a considerable simplification of many of the descriptors to enable any sensible comparison to be made of such items as frequency of surname, first name, or employment. This last has required the greatest simplification

Year	Surname	Entries	First	Entries	Occupation	Entries
1841	SMITH	73	Mary	200	Ag Lab	325
	BALDWIN	64	William	168	Domestic Servant	140
	STEVENS	49	John	153	Farmer	63
	TOMPSETT	49	Elizabeth	146	Lab	24
	WALLIS	49	James	127	Carpenter	13
	WEEKS	46	Thomas	114	Shoe Maker	12
	MANKTELOW	43	Sarah	111	Wheelwright	9
	KITCHENHAM	35	George	107	Bricklayer	8
	PACKHAM	32	Ann	97	Butcher	8
	PLAYSTED	32	Henry	74	Grocer	8
	different	371		201		64
1851	SMITH	109	Mary	228	Ag Lab	485
	WEEKS	65	William	203	Domestic Servant	155
	WALLIS	63	John	175	Farmer	68
	BALDWIN	41	Elizabeth	157	Rail Lab	55
	TOMPSETT	41	George	141	Lab	32
	PALMER	34	Thomas	128	Housekeeper	22
	STAPLEY	33	James	127	Bricklayer	19
	BLACKMAN	31	Sarah	99	Dressmaker	17
	KITCHENHAM	31	Ann	97	Cordwainer	16
	STEVENS	31	Harriett	63		
			Henry	63		
	different	445		214		109
1861	SMITH	81	Mary	200	Ag Lab	398
	TOMPSETT	43	William	171	Domestic Servant	92
	WALLIS	43	John	147	Farmer	61
	STYLES	42	Elizabeth	132	Carrier	47
	HUMPHREY	40	George	123	Housekeeper	26
	NEWINGTON	35	Thomas	112	Bricklayer	21
	WESTON	35	James	111	Carpenter	21
	BLACKMAN	34	Sarah	97	Blacksmith	13
	WEEKS	34	Ann	86	Shoe Maker	13
	BALDOCK	33	Henry	69	School Teacher	13
	different	390		205		120
1871	SMITH	103	Mary	238	Ag Lab	427
	MANKTELOW	62	William	210	Domestic servant	72
	TOMPSETT	53	George	167	Farmer	56
	STYLES	46	Elizabeth	162	Carpenter	40
	WALLIS	39	John	147	Bricklayer	31
	WEEKS	39	James	126	Gardener	25
	BLACKMAN	36	Thomas	120	Lab	23
	FAIRBROTHER	36	Sarah	114	Dressmaker	22
	BALDOCK	35	Ann	109	Housekeeper	22
	BALDWIN	35	Henry	80	Groom	20
	PATTENDEN	35				
	different	511		262		158

Year	Surname	Entries	First	Entries	Occupation	Entries
1881	SMITH	92	Mary	216	Ag Lab	398
	BALDWIN	52	William	209	Domestic Servant	95
	HUMPHREY	49	Elizabeth	157	Farmer	56
	TOMPSETT	47	George	150	Gardener	47
	PATTENDEN	44	John	127	Carpenter	38
	MANKTELOW	41	James	114	Lab	32
	WALLIS	41	Ann	111	Housekeeper	30
	WEEKS	35	Sarah	93	Dressmaker	25
	STYLES	34	Thomas	85	Bricklayers Lab	22
	KEMP	33	Charles	83	Grocer	21
	different	508		273		167
1891	SMITH	106	William	204	Ag Lab	395
	MANKTELOW	61	Mary	170	Domestic Servant	128
	PATTENDEN	50	George	166	Gardener	73
	BALDWIN	48	Elizabeth	149	Farmer	45
	WALLIS	48	John	121	Lab	43
	HUMPHREY	47	James	99	Carpenter	35
	NEWINGTON	33	Henry	95	Carrier	25
	TOMPSETT	33	Ann	94	Dressmaker	24
	BALDOCK	32	Charles	94	Grocer	24
	HEMSLEY	32	Frederick	85	Bricklayer	22
					Housekeeper	22
	different	562		288		150
1901	SMITH	92	William	192	Ag Lab	161
	MANKTELOW	54	Elizabeth	142	Domestic Servant	140
	TOMPSETT	48	George	139	Gardener	88
	HEMSLEY	43	Mary	131	Carrier	66
	WALLIS	36	Charles	111	Farmer	48
	HUMPHREY	32	Ann	106	Cook	47
	PATTENDEN	31	John	95	Stockman	46
	BALDWIN	30	Frederick	85	Carpenter	38
	NEWINGTON	28	Henry	85	Lab	33
	BALDOCK	27	Albert	77	Dressmaker	31
	LAVENDER	27			Groom	31
	different	608		307		173

because not only within each year's census but also between years, different enumerators have tended to use a variety of descriptors for what is essentially the same job of work: Agricultural Labourer, Ag Lab, Ag (Lab), Worker on Farm, Farm Boy, Farm Lab, Farm Labourer, Farm Labr, Farm servant, and Farmer's Son Working On Farm have therefore all been counted under the heading Ag Lab; the Stockman on farm and similar titles dealing with livestock, the Ag Lab (Carter), and Ag Lab Waggoners Mate have been counted separately.

Many other trades and professions are similarly confused - teachers, ministers of religion and doctors are some examples. In addition some census returns differentiate between grades within the trade - master, journeyman, clerk, assistant, apprentice. For the analysis which follows all these are counted within the trade, so the totals in the following table relate to trades rather than specific employments. Another complication is the inclusion in the Occupation heading of wives, sons, daughters, sisters and brothers: in some cases they are no doubt working with the person - usually a man - in the appropriate trade; inn keepers, post masters and several others; in other trades, they are probably not - wives and daughters were unlikely to work as bricklayers. In the tables, wives and others have generally been excluded from the totals.

The tables on the previous pages list for each census the 10 most frequently occurring names and occupations - where there is more than one in tenth place, all in that position are included. The underlying data are all held on spreadsheets so any further analysis can be readily undertaken.

Surname distribution

Excluding entries which cannot be clearly decipheredm and removing the uninhabited and unknown items, there are 20699 surname entries in the set. In every census year, Smith is the most common surname in the parish by a substantial margin in all years after 1841; Smith, Tompsett and Wallis appear in the top ten in all censuses. Baldwin and Newington feature in 6, Manktelow and Weeks in 5, Baldock, Humphrey and Pattenden in 4, Blackman and Styles in 3, Hemsley, Kitchenham and Stevens in 2, and Fairbrother, Kemp, Lavender, Packham, Palmer, Playsted, Stapley and Weston make a single appearance. This analysis is based on the spelling as used by the enumerators: names like Manktelow also appear as MANCKLOW, MANCTELOW, MANKELLOW, MANKELOW, MANKLOW, MANKTELLOW, MANKTELO - if these are all treated as one, then Manktelow would appear in second place in all census years. The increase in number of different surnames is steady over the years [except for 1851] - this can be linked to the general population growth.

First Names

In the analysis of frequency of first names, it seemed sensible to treat certain similar names as identical for the purposes of counting: the most obvious impact was to put Mary [including 99 instances of Maria and 2 of Marie over the 7 censuses] at the top of the lists for the years 1841 – 1881, second in 1891 and third in 1901; without that Mary would have featured in the top ten in all years but lower down. Similarly William benefited from the addition of Willm and Wm. Catherine [54 instances], Katherine [2 instances] and Kate [109 instances] were also treated as Catherine with no effect on the top ten; Ann [432 instances] had 30 instances of Anne, 46 of Anna and 191 of Annie added. To 786 instances of Elizabeth were added 261 of Eliza.

In the 1871 return there were 74 instances of Mary Ann and 15 of Mary A; in 1841 there were 26 entries for Mary Ann; in no other censuses did these combinations appear. This looked so much like an aberration, that I returned to the microfiche to check a significant sample - all had been correctly transcribed, so the figures were left to speak for themselves.

Mary and William share the two top places in all years except 1901 when Elizabeth creeps up to second place and George comes third. These four, together with Ann and John feature in every year; Henry and James appear in 6 out of the 7, Sarah and Thomas in 5, Charles in 3, Frederick in 2, and Albert - in 1901, and Harriet [or Harriett] - tenth equal in 1851, once each.

In looking at unusual first names, it cannot be assumed that all the enumerators spelled correctly but some of the following must have been correct:

Achsah	Adas	Adle
Crevoc	Efsby	Elwith
Estman	Keturah	Kohath
Louvaca	Nahoma	Obed
Persia	Phalec	Phezanna
Phishanna	Piolet	Sobyner
Tryphena	Zebulon	Zilpah

	Population	Houses	People/hhld
1841	2483	649	3.8
1851	2800	535	5.2
1861	2474	562	4.4
1871	3191	620	5.1
1881	3247	631	5.1
1891	3360	690	4.9
1901	3232	710	4.6

Population growth

Over the Victorian period, the population of Wadhurst did not change dramatically: an average of 5% a decade conceals two peaks - one in 1851 and another in 1891. If the 1841 census is ignored, the number of houses showed a steady increase over the rest of the period - some 33% over 60 years. Apart from a blip in 1861 the number of people living in each house fell slightly over the period, presumably reflecting greater prosperity and smaller families.

Occupations

8417 individuals out of the census total of 20800 had an entry against their name for occupation; some of these are retired and the total includes those who are living on their own means or declare themselves as 'Lady', 'Gentleman, 'Pauper' or 'On the Parish' etc.

Throughout the period, the agricultural labourer was predominant; only in 1901 is there a fall, from 395 in 1891 to 161 in 1901; this was not matched by a fall in the number of farmers, which show a small rise from 45 to 48. This probably reflects a shift to smaller holdings and less labour-intensive farming methods

Domestic service is the second most frequent occupation; the total is only of those whose occupation did not carry any distinctive label: there are also lady's maids, parlour maids, house boys and page boys and other relatively low-skilled workers in the house, as well as the more skilled - cooks and butlers for example. The totals in 1841 and 1901 are virtually the same - but the number of households has increased by a third, so the average number employed in each household has decreased.

There is a sudden appearance of railway labourers in 1851, marking the construction of the Tunbridge Wells to Hastings line through Wadhurst [*see page 85*]

Other Occupations

	1841	1851	1861	1871	1881	1891	1901
Artist			1			3	3
Attendant on Golf Links							1
Bill Poster							1
Banker						2	
Brick Maker	4	5	7	11	3	1	5
Bricklayer	8	19	21	31	20	22	28
Builder	2	1	5	18	22	9	27
Brickmaker's Lab		3	3	2	2	1	2
Builder			1	1	1	3	3
Builders Lab			1	3		1	1
Charcoal Burner						1	
Clergyman	2	3	4	6	8	8	8
Coffee House Manager					1		
Copper Smelter							1
Cordwainer	7	16	3	4	4		
Cripple					1		
Cycle Agent							1
Dental Surgeon							1
Electrical Engineer							2
Employed At Home		72		1			
Engine & Bicycle Fitter							1
Farmer	63	68	61	56	56	45	48
Farmer's Wife		1	11	9	14	1	3
Farmer's Son		4	22	21	14	10	16
Farmer's daughter			11	18	9		
Farmer's Widow		2					
Farmers Brother			1			3	2
Farmer's Sister			1				
Farm servant				16	8	13	
Gas Manager							1
Gas Stoker						2	

	1841	1851	1861	1871	1881	1891	1901
Hawker				1	2	4	2
Hay trusser				2	1	2	
Higgler	1	4	2				
Hoop Maker			2	2	3	8	10
Horse Jockey						1	
Hotwater Fitter (Gas)					1		
Illegitimate Da		1					
Laundress							30
Beer Retailer		8	5		2	2	1
Inn Keeper	5	5	8	7	10		
Licensed Victualler		2		1		5	8
Publican	4						2
Barmaid			2				
Mangle Woman					1		
Mineral Water Manufacture							1
Music Publisher							1
News agent							2
On Parish		2	1		1		10
Own Means	35	5	11	8	10	44	61
Pauper		38	4	5			
Queens Counsel						1	
Pupil Teacher		2		4	2		
School Teacher	3	8	13	8	18	16	17
Straw Bonnet Maker			3	1	2		
Tea Dealer					1		
Thrashing Machine Feeder						1	
Tinman						1	
Traction Engine Driver						2	
Visitor To The Sick (Missionary)					1		
Well Digger						1	3
Wood Blocker					1		

The tables above show some of the other changes in employment over the 60 years - some significant others simply interesting. The rise in the brick-related industry up to the 1880s is very marked, as is the arrival of new technologies - a cycle agent, an engine and bicycle fitter, a dental surgeon, two electrical engineers, a gas manager, a music publisher, and two newsagents in 1901. Other trades show a rise and fall - the cordwainer and the higgler.

Hoop making rises [hoops for what?] but straw bonnet makers only flourish in the middle decades.

Those 'on the parish' show a steep rise in 1901 but the declared paupers are only significant in 1851. Those declaring 'own means' show a fall in the middle years and a sharp rise in 1891 and 1901 as Victorian prosperity really takes root.

The full tables show many other interesting features and changes over the period but these will have to wait for a further publication. But what the analysis shows above all is the ease with which census data can be analysed once it is in spreadsheet form - and the errors that can creep in if real care is not taken at all times: for instance to a computer 'SMITH' is different to 'SMITH ' - one space after the name makes a real difference to a count or to an alphabetical sort!

Lodgers

From 1851, the 'Relation to Head of Household' was collected - this included a category of lodgers, their wives, sons and daughters. The table below shows a summary. There is a strong preponderance of agricultural labourers, none of whom lived with their farmer employer. Only in the 1851 census are

	1851	1861	1871	1881	1891	1901
No	148	53	84	71	65	36
Married	20	3	8	10	10	9
Widow/er	20	14	19	8	11	8
Unemployed	16 - all female	1	5	6	1	3
Occupations						
Ag Lab	45	27	30	18	17	16
Rail Lab	31					
Brick	5	4	9	5	4	
Ordnance Survey			8			
Hawkers					4	
under 14	14			1		1
Pauper dwarf						
In barn						

there significant numbers of children shown as lodgers; after that, one has to assume that there was sufficient rented accommodation available for those who had families.

The agricultural labourers almost invariably lodged with a fellow labourer, although towards the end of the period, the local inns began to take in larger numbers of lodgers of all sorts.

The return for 1851 also shows as lodgers 1 pauper dwarf and 1 'in barn'.

The age of the population

The final analysis shows the age ranges of the population over this census period. Ages were recorded for all 7 returns - and for 20789 of the total 20800 entries in the censuses. For 1841, ages tended to be entered in bands over the age of 5 but some enumerators continued to put down a precise age. For the

	1841	1851	1861	1871	1881	1891	1901
under 1	77	50	35	103	97	56	71
1-5	401	428	386	489	486	435	342
6-10	360	384	317	391	439	439	355
11-14	224	252	227	284	292	325	283
15-20	402	303	300	354	319	379	370
21-30	360	431	295	517	465	460	533
31-40	250	355	280	328	391	411	402
41-50	166	257	243	272	258	337	355
51-60	126	160	195	209	234	225	238
61-70	74	114	112	142	147	179	164
71-80	32	48	59	85	67	79	96
over 80	9	18	21	17	21	24	23
totals	2481	2800	2470	3191	3216	3349	3232

purposes of this analysis, ages over 1 have been shown in bands; those aged 20 and under have been grouped as under 1, 1-5, 6-10, 11-14 [an age when all except the wealthier or brighter were sent to work] and 15-20. There were few over 90 so they have been included in the over 80 group.

1841   85   Benjamin Baldwin, agricultural labourer
1851   94   Elizabeth Hoadly, widow
1861   91   William Bassett, widower, agricultural labourer
1871   95   Francis Manktelow, married to Ash [aged 85], with a son an agricultural labourer, aged 51 unmarried and living with his parents
1881   91   Joseph Kine, widower, retired farmer - being looked after by his three unmarried daughters: Mary - 52, Elisabeth - 51, and Martha - 46
1891   96   Esther Fairway, widow, living on own means
1901   91   Hilary Bishop, widower, retired gardener - with his widowed daughter Mary Brissenden [66] as his housekeeper

Several points can be drawn out from the figures. A decline in the number of children under the age of 10 could suggest a reduction in the size of families over the period - something for later analysis. There are considerable increases in the older age groups, surely reflecting better health for all and, in particular, the improvements in children's health over the first part of the census period.

The age of the oldest resident does not show any obvious pattern, except that they were all over 90 after 1841 - and that five were men and only 2 women; and, of the men, all worked outdoors.

	1841	1851	1861	1871	1881	1891	1901
under 1	3.1	1.8	1.4	3.2	3.0	1.7	2.2
1-5	16.2	15.3	15.6	15.3	15.1	13.0	10.6
6-10	14.5	13.7	12.8	12.3	13.7	13.1	11.0
11-14	9.0	9.0	9.2	8.9	9.1	9.7	8.8
15-20	16.2	10.8	12.1	11.1	9.9	11.3	11.4
21-30	14.5	15.4	11.9	16.2	14.5	13.7	16.5
31-40	10.1	12.7	11.3	10.3	12.2	12.3	12.4
41-50	6.7	9.2	9.8	8.5	8.0	10.1	11.0
51-60	5.1	5.7	7.9	6.5	7.3	6.7	7.4
61-70	3.0	4.1	4.5	4.5	4.6	5.3	5.1
71-80	1.3	1.7	2.4	2.7	2.1	2.4	3.0
over 80	0.4	0.6	0.9	0.5	0.7	0.7	0.7
totals	2481	2800	2470	3191	3216	3349	3232

Population by age, shown as a percentage of the total population in the year

Most of the trends can more readily seen from the table above, which makes allowance for the changes in population and for the 33% increase between 1841 and 1901 by converting the totals above into percentages. Now the increase in the older age groups is more obvious - the over 80s increase from 0.4% of the population to 0.7% and the 41-50 group from 6.7% to 11%.

The figures for 1841, 1871 and 1881 for the under one year olds show as a much higher percentage of the population than the other four sets of census data: the reason is not apparent from the census information but what is clear is that those born in 1841 had a much lower rate of survival to the age of ten. Taking those born in 1841 [3.1% of the population] and 1881 [1.8%], ten years later the 6-10 age group represented 13.7% [1841] and 12.8% [1851] of the census populations, surely suggesting higher mortality rates for those born in the earlier years.

Conclusions

Census returns are an addictive area for study and much more can be gleaned about Wadhurst's Victorian past than is presented here. The information above presents a snapshot across the whole parish of Wadhurst as it was between 1841 and 1901. The key features are the steady growth in population and the shift from an agricultural society towards a more industrial [in a loose sense of the word] and commercial one.

SOURCES

Census returns for the years between 1841 and 1901, the originals of which are held in the National Archives, Kew

FARMING AND FORESTRY IN VICTORIAN TIMES
MARTIN TURNER

Hardship and Unrest Leading up to the Reign of Queen Victoria.

The years immediately preceding the Victorian period were very difficult for farming. Between 1816 and 1842 there was considerable agricultural distress following the Napoleonic wars when large numbers of men were discharged from the armed services. These men then swamped the rural labour market. Corn prices dropped from a high level between 1796 to 1815, this in turn caused farmers to make severe cuts at the expense of their labourers. The introduction of mechanisation and particularly the hated threshing machine took away much needed employment, leading to riots and burnings by village labourers, demanding higher pay, during the 1830-32 period. There is no evidence of this occurring in Wadhurst Parish nor of the burning of hay ricks and farm buildings which occurred at this time in neighbouring areas of the Weald and elsewhere. There were no trade unions to help or hinder in that period. The event of the Tolpuddle martyrs happened in 1834, but it was some years later before a trade union was formed for agricultural workers.

What had made these years particularly taxing was that much of the land had become sterile through over cropping during wartime and this land had not completely recovered for lack of farmer's capital to improve it. Then shortly followed three wet seasons in 1816, 1817 and 1821, which not only had made the land almost unworkable but had led to widespread foot rot which had wiped out sheep flocks. George Smallpiece a farmer land agent, broker and sheep dealer, when giving evidence to the Select Committee on Agriculture in 1833 exclaimed "I would not have the whole Weald to farm if they would give it to me".

What made the post Napoleonic depression exceptionally testing was the requirement to pay regularly, in cash, the high poor rates then prevailing in Wealden parishes.

Wealden parishes had seen a marked growth in the number of persons dependent on Parish relief during the late 18th and early 19th centuries. The charge fell on all occupiers of land roughly in proportion to the acreage held, so small farmers paid less than large ones. These poor rates rose substantially after 1822. However larger farmers were in a sense also beneficiaries, for each summer many employed a number of casual labourers whom they could let the parish support during the winter. Small farms worked largely by family labour gained little from this pool of casual labour yet were still required to contribute to parish relief. The high poor rates induced some farmers to leave the parish when their leases expired. As a result their land was left in a wretched state of cultivation.

In his book *The Kent and Sussex Weald*, Peter Brandon says "given fair land, a man his wife and four to six children needed a minimum of about 50 acres to make a living during this period." However it is apparent that there were several, maybe many, farms of smaller acreage than this. The present acreage comprising Little Pell for example, was made up of Great Pell being about 85 acres, Little Pell of about 70 acres as well as Pell Bottom and Walters Farms of about 21 and 31 acres apiece. The very small farms were in all probability worked by the wife whose husband was employed on a larger farm or some timber enterprise, for example. The small farm would have had a sow, reared some pigs, kept a few cows, had a calf or two, maintained an area for potatoes and vegetables and had some grazing land. Poultry also played a large part in helping farmers through difficult times. It was said that a smallholder with poultry was often better off than a larger farm without. In the 1851 census 40% of those in employment worked in agriculture.

Farmers would also have sown a few acres of corn and no doubt used the Cousley Wood windmill[1] and Bartley Mill water mill, to make their flour. In the winter farmers from the Marshes drove sheep up into the Weald to graze, just as pigs had been in earlier times to feast in winter on acorns. This may have supplemented the income of some of the larger farms. The origin of the name Shovers Green is thought to have come from the time when the drovers were active over the winter months.

By 1839 there were 3,200 acres of arable under cultivation in the parish and 3,100 acres of meadow and pasture. Meadow presumably included fields being rested in the normal course of rotation. By comparison, there were only about 750 acres under the plough in the parish in 1988.

The traditional Wealden cattle farming system involved the retention of all male calves which were then used as plough oxen between the ages of three and six, followed by fattening for the butcher.

The farmers found the abundant supply of manure, from the winter stall fed cattle, very beneficial for their hop farms. As the nineteenth century progressed, horses replaced oxen as plough animals on many farms and the emphasis of the cattle economy had shifted towards rearing and dairying.

The smaller Wealden farmer sold only as much produce as was necessary to support his simple life style.

One innovation, which although invented in about 1824 by a man in Perthshire did not come to the Weald until considerably later, was the subsoil plough. It was particularly beneficial to the heavy Weald soil. By the use of this plough wet land, which before had proved hopeless for cultivation, be-

---

[1] The Cousley Wood windmill was sold in 1819 "in full trade" and was then let to a miller Mr Holmwood. The Bartley Mill was in operation for the whole of the 19th century.

came reasonably mellow and friable. This plough stirred the subsoil without raising it to the surface thus giving a much greater depth for the rain to sink into. The way it was used was that an ordinary plough went first and turned over a furrow six to eight inches deep and the subsoil plough followed behind in the same track to a further depth of 12 to 16 inches.

A Wadhurst ploughing contest at the turn of the century

Boys were expected to take up daily work on farms as soon as they had the strength to work the stiff cold clay, usually about the age of 10 or 11. Peter Brandon in his book tells the story of one Thomas Orton, living in the Weald, but exact place not known, who had just had his 12th birthday in 1836 when he spoke of his 12 hour day, leading the horse with his father at the plough and harrow and doing other jobs according to season. For meals he had bread and cheese or bread and butter for breakfast and sometimes, but not often, bread and meat and potatoes for dinner. Bread was very much the staple diet for the agricultural labourer. The nine children, five boys and four girls slept in one room. He had attended school for only one week and could not read. He admitted that few were as badly off. Until that age most had an irregular education in a Dame or other local school, punctuated by spells of bird scaring, potato and bean sowing and acorn collecting.

"Plodding along at a jog trot to the local rail-head, a running commentary would be heard from old labourers recalling the time when grazing land, piece by piece, replaced the plough and where first the horses had ousted the immemorial ox teams [see page 23]".

Many small farmers undertook seasonal work on larger farms both local and in other regions such as the South Downs or in the wood coppice industries. Farmers with small acreage were not therefore necessarily those with the smallest incomes.

In 1840 Thomas Carlyle, travelling through Sussex on his way to Herstmonceux, reported that, although farming was depressed, farmers struggled to keep wages at 12 shillings a week as a point of honour, based on a general understanding that a man could not keep a family under that wage.

Until the 1830s to 1840s when the Excise men became better staffed with soldiers returning from the Napoleonic wars, smuggling would almost undoubtedly have been a part of the income of some farmers. After all they had the horses, the men and the buildings and Wadhurst was within a night's ride of the coast.

Out of interest, the Tomsett family, who had farmed Holbeam Wood just to the north of the Ticehurst road from the early 1700s until 1886, were also known to have had interests in London; would it be pure conjecture to associate all this with smuggling? Incidentally in 1818 a map of the 247 acre Holbeam Wood Farm was made. This map shows the fields then being farmed to be almost identical to what they are today, with only about 4 acres more woodland than there are at present; the fields are also all named the same.

The Hop Industry

The acreage under cultivation for hops had been growing in Wadhurst from the 18th century when the acreage at that time had been 457 acres. During the difficult times for farmers in the early years of Victoria's reign, hop farmers did better than those dependent on meat and corn. By 1839 the acreage under hops had reached 617. Proof of this increasing importance are the three identical oast houses built by the Whiligh Estate at Little Pell, Little Brissenden and Beaumans in 1852, 1853 and 1854. Each oast had two kilns of 11' 6" diameter. Production continued to increase and was further stimulated by the abolition of heavy duty on hops in 1862. A further oast was built at Nomanswood on the Stonegate road in 1880. This had two kilns of 16' 6" in diameter and must have been an excellent oast for the period as the draught would have been very good. By the end of the century the acreage under hops had reached 1,885.

Because of disease and pests, hops could never be a staple crop for the farmer, hence the saying-

"Until St James (July 25th) be come and gone
there may be hops there may be none"

(Does the origin of the name St James' Square in the middle of Wadhurst stem from this?) Spraying hops did not start until about 1890 in the Weald.

The unreliability of hops is also shown in an old Kentish verse which includes the lines:

"First the flea then the fly
Then the mould and then they die"

In a good year, hops were profitable and provided the jam on the bread and butter. They were labour intensive, but labour was cheap: men very often worked from six in the morning to six at night Monday to Saturday for a shilling a day. The skilled work of hop-tying was carried out by women on piece rates; they would do well to make more than two pence an hour. When it came to picking it was nearly all piece work. The rate set was known as the 'tally', that is the number of bushels to the shilling, the picker being given a 'tally' after each 'measure', showing the amount picked. At this time the tally was usually 7 or 8, depending on the size of the hops. It would be an exceptional picker who would pick 3 bushels an hour; the average would be perhaps 2. Thus with a tally of 8, the average picker would earn, in a ten hour day, the sum of 2 shillings and sixpence. An acre would yield perhaps 10 cwt, or say 1,000 bushels, representing £6-5-0 in pickers' wages.

Little Pell Farm - Jabez Smith at the bin

Sussex hops did not command quite as good a price as hops from Kent and when in 1894 the county boundaries were redrawn, Lamberhurst which had been partly in Kent and partly in Sussex, with the River Teise as the boundary, opted to become part of Kent rather than Sussex, for this reason.

Forestry

Woodland was important to the well-being of the farmer. The pedunculate or common oak which grows so readily in the Weald - and is therefore often known as the Sussex weed - was very highly favoured for ship building, more so than the slower growing sessile oak. 1000 acres of oak were required to maintain the Navy as it was then, for just one year. A 74 gun ship (only a third rater) would require 2000 large well-grown oak trees, stripping at least 50 acres of wood, and nearly twice that amount for a 120 gun first rate ship.

The demand for ship timbers declined dramatically from the late 1840s. A further blow for the timber trade came in 1846 with the removal of import duty on imported timber and yet another in 1850 with the repeal of the Navigation Acts. Up until that time goods had to be carried in British built merchant ships, but from 1850 our merchant ships could be built abroad. The slow-down in ship building also affected the need for the teams of oxen and men required to drag the timber to the ship-building yards. This could take as much as two years, since during the height of winter loads might be abandoned when tracks became too deep in impassable mud.

The building of HMS Warrior in 1862 signalled the demise of the "wooden walls" and the turnover to ironclads. The value of every kind of woodland declined from the late 1870s with increased imports of timber and the substitution of other materials for wood. This blow fell mainly on the larger landowners who were simultaneously having to reduce rents. There was no incentive to convert the chestnut coppice woodlands which had been in existence since the 16th century to high forest. Any sense of urgency to grow timber soon evaporated.

This was to prove a factor in the break up of estates from 1900; it also had a disastrous effect on rural employment and on the small farmer. In the Weald, the underwood industry had furnished a vast field of employment from October to May by felling timber, cutting coppice for hop poles and fencing, shaving hoops, splitting wattles, basket making and binding faggots. Men earned high wages at this time but the industry was virtually at its end by the early 1900s. This had severe effects on the small farmer and cottager, the key to his prosperity being these supplementary sources of income, especially in winter when his land was more or less idle. The vanishing presence of the small farm can be traced to the failure of one after the other of these side sources.

These various setbacks soon left marks of decay on the landscape. Some land in the 1880s and 1890s, which had been under cultivation, was tumbling down into good-for-nothing pasture. On particularly poor strips, land was allowed to slip back to its natural aspect of oak saplings, 6 foot high bracken and bramble. Even on better land there were poor thistly pastures and half tilled fields. The miller now only ran the stones at the watermill for half the time of 20 years earlier.

The Whiligh Ledgers

Much fascinating information concerning farming life can be gleaned from the "Whiligh Ledgers" which were kept by the Courthope Estate, from 1825 to 1891. All these ledgers, with the exception of the one for the period 1868 to 1873, kept at Whiligh, are held in the Records Office at Lewes. In these ledgers, every week is represented on an A2 size sheet. Some facts and examples from the 1863-1868 ledger are shown below:

* WHAT EVERY EMPLOYEE DID ON EACH DAY IS SHOWN FOR THE SIX WORKING DAYS OF THE WEEK. THE COURTHOPE LAND COMPRISED ABOUT 3,000 ACRES OF WHICH OVER 600 WERE WOODLAND.

* THERE WERE NEVER LESS THAN 25 EMPLOYEES, SOME PART TIME. THIS DID NOT INCLUDE THOSE EMPLOYED IN THE GARDEN PROBABLY ABOUT SIX.

* ABOVE EVERY DAY, THE WEATHER ON THAT DAY IS SHOWN.

* JOHN NEWINGTON THE SENIOR FOREMAN RECEIVED £1-2-0 PER WEEK FOR THE FIRST RECORDED WEEK IN THE LEDGER, AND EXACTLY THE SAME FOR THE LAST RECORDED WEEK, 4 YEARS LATER.

* THE TOTAL WEEK'S WAGES FOR THE 25 EMPLOYEES IN THE FIRST WEEK WAS £15-15-0. A FURTHER £4-14-6 WAS PAID TO ONE HILARY BISHOP, TO PAY TO THE GARDENERS.

* SOME OTHER STILL LOCAL NAMES APPEARING, ARE HENRY AND EDWARD TOMPSETT, JOHN AND JAMES MANKTELOW.

* ENTRY FOR GOOD FRIDAY 1869 - "ALL MEN NOT MARKED WITH A CROSS ATTENDED DIVINE SERVICE AND ARE PAID FOR THE DAY". (THE SAME FOR CHRISTMAS DAY.) - i.e.. no church = no pay!

* FRIDAY AUGUST 5TH 1870 - "HARVEST HOME THE WORKMEN ALL ATTEND AND ARE PAID FOR THE DAY."

* IF A MAN WAS SICK HE DID NOT NORMALLY RECEIVE ANY PAY.

* WASHING SHEEP AT 6d PER SCORE (1869)

* TWO EMPLOYEES SPENT 2 DAYS SOWING CHESTNUTS IN THE NURSERY.

* ATTENDING TO COWS ON THE LAWN

* COALS FROM STATION

* TAKING CATTLE TO MARKET IN TONBRIGE [*sic*] (Tonbridge was the nearest market. The Wadhurst cattle market was opened in the 1890s.)

There are several entries mentioning cider making and assisting with brewing.

Marl

By the time Queen Victoria came to the throne, the practice of marling had largely died out with the increasing availability of lime for fertilising the arid Wealden soil; described as having a rubber like quality in winter and concrete hardness in summer. But since ancient marl pits are in such evidence in our local landscape and because of the author's fascination with the subject, this note about marl is added.

The Weald farmer was by necessity manure mad; he fed the lean soil as a farmer might cram a chicken before marketing. Dung, compost, sleech (ditch diggings) and seaweed were all used. However unquestionably the cornerstone of Wealden farming for at least six centuries was marling. The arrival of the railway enabled woollen rags from London to be used on the hop fields as manure. This was done every three years or so. The rags were spread at about 1 ton per acre at a cost of £5 per ton.

By definition marl is a crumbly mixture of clay, sand and limestone. Marl ploughed into Wealden soil added substance, improved the ability of the soil to absorb water and added a measure of fertilisation.

The readiest method of marling, where calcareous strata was at hand, was to open a pit at the corner of a field. The underlying bed of calcareous clay was then winched up in buckets and liberally spread and ploughed in to enrich the soil. In some areas one or two pits centrally placed were dug to serve the whole area and with repeated use over the centuries became yawning holes "deep enough to down the weathercock on a church steeple and wide enough to accommodate the church as well." In Wadhurst parish we have examples of such pits with 'The Marlpit' between Durgates and Sparrows Green and an equally large marl pit near Pell Green.

In the 13th century marl was regarded as so essential to Wealden tillage that some landlords had written into the farm lease that every field should be heavily marled once in a generation. There is an example from 1347 when eleven and a half acres were dressed with marl by 7 men and 6 boys taking 8 weeks. In the late 13th century land that had recently been marled was worth three times land which had not been. Other examples indicate that fields were more frequently marled and that this needed to be done after every three or four sowings of corn.

Not all our many pits, scattered over the parish and now very often filled with water, can be said to be old marl pits, since the sandstone underlying the clay was also dug up for building houses and for strengthening the tracks across the land which during the winter months would otherwise have been impassable. Other pits may also have been diggings for iron ore or even where the odd German V1 rocket crashed.

Working the Wealden clay with a team of oxen in the 1890s

SOURCES

Peter Brandon: *The Kent and Sussex Weald* Phillimore 2003

Alan Savidge and Oliver Mason: *Wadhurst - Town of the High Weald* Meresborough Press 1998

E.J. Hobsbawn and G. Rude: *Captain Swing* Lawrence & Wishart 1969

Esmond and Jean Harris: *Oak a British History* Windgather Press 2003

N.D.G.James: *A History of English Forestry* Blackwell 1981

H.R.Haggard :*Rural England vol 1 pages 104-136* Longmans, Green 1902

The Whiligh Ledgers - ESRO and John Hardcastle

East Sussex Record Office, Lewes

Comment and input also provided by Messrs John Hardcastle, Peter Mulleneux and Jim Overy

THE DEVELOPMENT OF VICTORIAN WADHURST BETWEEN THE TURNPIKE GATES

RACHEL RING

"The Town, properly so called, is in length 5 or 6 furlongs, reckoning from the Castle Gate, to the Lower Turnpike; about mid-way between these two points, a slight diverging of the main street, forming what is called the Middle Row, communicates on the west by several narrow ways, and on the east a broad open space."

Extract taken from William Courthope's collection
at the College of Arms vol 26 (circa 1840)

LEISURE

What is this life if, full of care,
We have no time to stand and stare?
No time to stand beneath the bough
And stare as long as sheep or cows.
No time to see, when woods we pass
Where squirrels hid their nuts in grass.

No time to see, in broad daylight,
Streams full of stars like skies at night.
No time to turn at Beauty's glance,
And watch her feet, how they can dance.
No time to wait till her mouth can
Enrich that smile her eyes began.

A poor life this if, full of care,
We have no time to stand and stare.

This was written by W.H. Davies who was born right in the middle of Queen Victoria's reign and, as his words were so apt for us during our "looking, reading and writing" periods over the past year, we felt it would be good to share it. Had we not taken the time to "stand and stare" at the High Street area, it is possible we would have missed much of the heritage being studied. Hopefully, all of us will heed these poignant words and use our eyes well and take the time to "stand and stare" more often.

Wadhurst in the 1880s - the half timbered building on the left was pulled down 1888 and the current building erected. Sheepwash Lane is further on and then the Queen's Head

The area studied falls between the two central tollgates; one of which was on the main road outside the Primary School and the other just past the Youth Centre in the Lower High Street.

The main source of our findings comes from the census records of 1841 through to 1901 and analysis of the spreadsheets we produced of the information contained in these records. We have no reason to believe that our general findings would not have been replicated throughout the parish, but due to time restrictions only the main thoroughfare has been researched.

Three major building projects undertaken during Victoria's reign in the High Street were the Wesleyan/Methodist Chapel in 1874, the National School in 1856 (now the Youth Centre) and the Baptist Chapel (now Crittles) in about 1866. However, the old timbered property where Gobles/Jackie Martel now stands was demolished in 1888 and the present property erected approximately three years later.

The remainder of the research has been from books covering the period, the internet in relation to the Poor Law and the formation of Unions and numerous full day visits to the East Sussex Record Office in Lewes where so many of the local records are now held. Our thanks are due to all the staff there for their help.

Occupations / Employment in the High Street 1841 – 1901

Rosemary Pope

This analysis covers the census returns from 1841 to 1901, the whole of Queen Victoria's reign. It has been limited to the Wadhurst High Street between the tollgates.

Summary of Information Taken from Census Returns 1841-1901							
	1841	1851	1861	1871	1881	1891	1901
Population in Area	429	472	437	456	461	460	477
65 Years or Over	12	21	22	29	32	36	24
14 Years or Younger	176	165	157	123	140	116	112
Born in Village	nr	278	245	232	241	252	109
Born in Frant, Mayfield, Ticehurst or Lamberhurst	nr	41	37	41	37	31	40
Households	~ 100	91	101	96	97	103	100

nr not recorded in census

Labouring employed the greatest number of males. This includes agricultural labouring and in 1851 railway labourers during the construction of the railway period. Numbers ranged from 40 in 1851 to 21 in 1891. The oldest labourer appears to be George Cavey aged 78 in 1871 and the youngest was James Attwood aged 13 in 1851. However, several labourers were in their 70s and boys of 14 were commonly marked on the returns as labourers.

Servants: these numbers ranged from 18 in 1881 to 41 in 1891. This may be accounted for by a) the occupation of Wadhurst Castle and b) the opening of several larger shops e.g. John Greenhill grocer and draper who employed four assistants, or apprentices, and three servants to look after his family and the assistants and apprentices. Most of the servants were female and some

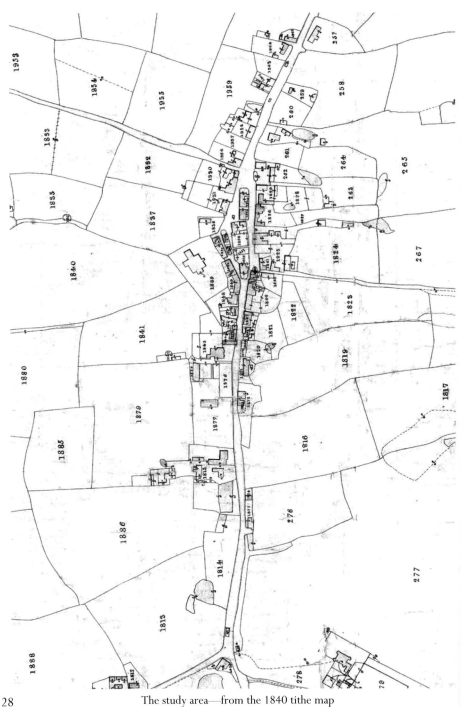

The study area—from the 1840 tithe map

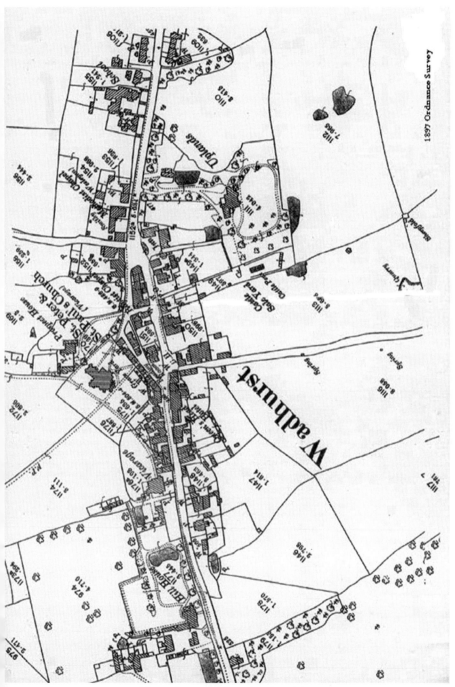

The study area—from the 1897 OS map

seem to be servants in their own family. For example, Almenia Benge, aged 12 years in 1891. She had six younger siblings but could have been living at home and working as a daily maid elsewhere. It appears that the town becomes more prosperous over the period as more servants are employed in one household with specific duties, e.g. housemaid, parlour maid, as opposed to the one maid of all work. Some moved to the town with the family employing them e.g. the Boyd family whose servants all came from Durham where their son Edward Boyd was born.

Jabez Smith's Saddlery and harness making premises around 1870. He ran this business for many years before operating the postal service from the same site. Story has it that the premises were Tudor in origin and that it was the **old** Queen's Head until it closed around 1840 when Jabez set up his business. After demolition in 1888 two new houses were erected on the site, from which the saddlery and post office were again operated.

Building Trades included here are bricklayers (brick and tile making), carpenters, plumbers and painters.

Builders, especially bricklayers, were busy throughout the period. However, the number of households remained the same (see table on page 27) so where were the bricks being laid? Sparrows Green and Cousley Wood were expanding also other out-lying areas so possibly their work took them there. The highest number of bricklayers occurs in 1861 but why? It has been ascertained that the railway construction was not the reason.

Blacksmiths: A steady number of blacksmiths are shown throughout the period, two, three or four, but dominated by two families, Reed and Page/Pilbeam. William Reed was a blacksmith in 1851, 1861, 1871 and 1881 when he was 74 years old. David Page appears in 1871 as a blacksmith/journeyman and in 1881 and 1891 was entered just as a blacksmith. In 1901 he has retired and is living with his daughter and son-in-law, Tom Pilbeam, also a blacksmith. His son, also Tom, retired from the business next to the Methodist Church about 1940 and his daughter Dorothy Edwards still lives in the town.

Work with leather including saddler, cordwainer, harness maker, shoemaker/bootmaker and currier.

The currier master only appears in 1851 and in 1871. If the cordwainers and shoemakers are combined there appears to be at least a dozen working at this trade during the period. A reminder again here that this particular survey is only concentrating on the High Street between the two Toll Gates! The family of Pilbeam were involved in 1851, 1871, 1881, and 1891.

Turn of the century High Street

There were one or two saddlers working throughout the period except in 1891 when we find there were four harness makers shown although this probably included saddlery.

Clothes making including tailors, dressmakers, milliners and hatmaker.

Tailoring was a male occupation often passing from father to son; Hamilton in 1841 to 1881, Ashby 1851 to 1871, Burt 1851 to 1871 and Howard 1881 to 1901. Some had apprentices or employees e.g. Noakes in 1851.

High Street - Couchman's chemists and veterinary shop on the right

Millinery/bonnet making disappeared in 1881; Mary Mott, straw bonnet maker [aged 65] had her daughter Alma as a dressmaker. Another interesting person is Mary Ann Burt who changed from being a milliner to a dressmaker and continued until 1901. It is suspected that she was related to Burt the tailor (1851 to 1871) but this assumption cannot be verified by the census returns.

Dressmaking was again a family occupation; Mary Ann Burt had three nieces working with her and a boarder in 1901. Two Benge sisters were working together in 1901 and mother and daughter Baldock in 1871. The impression is that dressmakers often lived near to each other e.g. Daws and Baldock families and in 1851 Baley and Maryan at 1 and 2 Market Street.

Shops - including grocers, bakers, butchers and drapers.

In the early years odd combinations of occupations appear, e.g. in 1851 Wisdom ran a beer shop and was also a butcher and in 1861 Carpenter was a head bricklayer and a baker, his wife was also a baker. John Mackdonald (later spelt Macdonald) from Scotland opens a grocer's shop in 1841; by 1851 it is a grocers/drapers and he is employing a shopman and again in 1861. He has disappeared in 1871 but O T Corke is running a grocers/drapers with five assistants. In 1881 Maria Macdonald, daughter of the above John, is back as a grocer/draper employing two men and one boy. She was still in Wadhurst in 1891 employing three but is not on the census return for 1901 when she would have been 70 years old. Meanwhile, O T Corke is progressing in 1881 as he is employing eight men in his shop in St James' Square, similarly in 1891 and in1901 his son Harry has taken over with seven assistants.

High Street around the turn of the century - Newington's on the left

If we follow the Carpenter family (bakers) in 1871 - Charles is now a Master Baker and employing two of his sons as bakers. He is still working in 1881 but has died by 1891, his widow continuing the business. In 1901 the son Alfred is in charge with one assistant baker.

There appears to be a change during the period to larger shops often continued over two or three generations. Examples have been given of bakers and grocers. Looking at butchers, there is the Smith family; in 1861 Jabez aged 42, and his son Alfred, are employing one assistant. In 1871 the younger son Rowland has taken Alfred's place and is now master butcher aged 25; his father Jabez is the postmaster. By 1881 Rowland is also a farmer employing a butcher and a boy. By 1891 he has three assistants. In 1901, now a widower, he has two sons working with him as butchers and a daughter as a clerk. Henry Fillery appears for the first time in 1901 as another butcher in the Town and is already employing his son, aged 13, and two others in his business.

<u>Watchmaker – Clockmaker</u> One family kept this trade continuing from 1841 to 1901. According to the census returns, in 1841 Owen Newington was shown and again in 1851; by 1861 Owen is joined by his eldest son Horace who continues on his own in 1871 and 1881. In 1891 Horace is a tobacconist

but in 1901 son Harry is a watchmaker. (Harry remained a clocksmith until the 1930s).

<u>Inn Keepers – Beer seller</u> After all this work the town needed refreshment!

Three pubs (inns) are mentioned throughout the period - the Queen's Head, the White Hart and the Greyhound. In 1851 the White Hart is run by George Wilkinson, innkeeper and butchers; in 1861 Sam Tooth of the Queen's Head is also a coal merchant. By 1891 the name innkeeper is being replaced by licensed victualler. In 1881 the White Hart takes in lodgers, and in 1901 Charles Tompsett has 13 lodgers but the inn's name is not given; however, it is not the Greyhound. Jacob Pitt has been innkeeper there from 1861 to 1881, having started work at the Vine in Cousle Wood [*sic*] in 1841, working for his father Abram; in 1901 Jacob's son Harry is shown as a licenced victualler in 'Town' - by inference the Greyhound.

The Queen's Head

Analysis

The town appears a very busy community during the period 1841 to 1901 and all the basic needs are catered for. General prosperity increases, note the larger shops developing and the inhabitants of independent means in 1891 and 1901 [*see the table on page 11*].

Between 1851 and 1901 there are only three or four households employing several indoor servants. One is Hill House (Wace until 1891). There is also the vicarage, the home of the village doctor and Prospect House (now The Lodge). Wadhurst Castle is just outside the survey area. Tradesmen employed an indoor maid and sometimes an outdoor servant, usually male, when the shops became larger.

Occupations that disappear during the period of the survey

Tollgate Keeper	1871 last mention
Shepherd	1871 last mention
Police inspector	1851 first and last mention- railway construction period?
Railway labourers	1851 only mention
Inspector of railways	1851 only mention
Millwright	1841 only mention
Gunsmith	1861 last mention
Chain maker	1841 last mention
Cooper	1861 last mention

Entries are not shown which could be under another name/title

Occupations that appear to be new during the period

Auctioneer	1891 and 1901
Bookseller/Newsagent	1901
Chimney sweep	1891 and 1901
Parish Clerk	1891 (1888/1894 Act to set up Parish Councils)
Cycle Agent	1901
Greengrocer and Florist	1901
Porter	1901
JP	1901
Lodging House Keeper	1901
Mail Contractor HM	1901
Organist	1901
Page	1901
Police Constable	1881, 1891 and 1901
Telegraph boy	1901
Postman (4)	1901
Tobacconist	1891
Undertaker	1891

Comments

Population figures show a fairly stable town. Increase in numbers in 1851 probably are due to the workers on the railway construction who lodged in the town and had moved on by 1861.

POST OFFICE DIRECTORY 1855

WADHURST is a large parish, about six miles from Tunbridge Wells, seventeen from Battle, 33 from Hastings, and 22 from Rye; in Loxfield Pelham hundred, Pevensey rape, and Ticehurst union. It has a station on the Tunbridge and Hastings Railway; and in 1851 there were 2802 inhabitants. The church is an interesting structure, and the interior contains several ancient monuments and brasses. The living is a vicarage, in the patronage of Wadham College, Oxford; the Rev. John A. Foley, M.A., is the incumbent. The Wesleyans and Baptists have each a chapel in the village.

POST OFFICE.—Jabez Smith, Postmaster. Letters arrive at 8 a.m., and are despatched at 7 p.m. Money Orders are granted and paid.

Carr, John, esq. Gate house
Crouch, Rev. William, Baptist
Dixon, Henry, esq. Frank house
Foley, Rev. John, M.A. Vicar, Vicarage
Goble, Iden, esq. Hightown
Jones, Rev. James
Mercer, William, esq.
Newington, Joseph John, esq. Towgate
Smith, Mr. John
Smith, Mr. Joseph
Smyth, Edw. Watson, esq. Wadhurst castle
Wace, Richard Henry, esq. Legases

Apps, William, turner
Arnold, William, farmer
Ashby, William, miller
Austen, Henry Jeffery, farmer and auctioneer
Austen, Thomas, farmer and appraiser
Avery, William, farmer
Baldwin, Charles, butcher
Ballard, Thomas, blacksmith
Ballard, John, Old Vine inn
Barham, Alfred, wheelwright
Barham, Eastman, wheelwright and farmer
Barham, Nicholas, wheelwright
Barton, Thomas, farmer
Bean, William, farmer
Benge, James, farmer
Boarer, John, Sportsman inn, and farmer
Bocking, Charles, National schoolmaster
Bone, James, shoemaker
Brissenden, Charles, farmer
Burt, James, tailor
Carpenter, Charles, shopkeeper
Cheeseman and Co. drapers, grocers, and tailors
Couchman, Thomas, veterinary surgeon and druggist
Orundwell, Stephen, farmer

Dadswell, Edwin, hairdresser
Dadswell, John, beer retailer
Descon, Peter, station master
Davis, John, carpenter
Fairbrother, James, weaver
Fairbrother, John, brickmaker
Fairbrother, Samuel, beer retailer
Fuggle, Misses F. and G. ladies' school
Fry, George, Red Lion, and farmer
Gallup, George, blacksmith
Gibb, Henry, wheelwright
Gibb, Samuel, farmer
Golds, Alfred, shopkeeper
Hammond, Edward, butcher and innkeeper
Hammond, John, cooper
Hammond, Thomas, cooper
Harmer, James, farmer
Hemsley, Sarah Ann, farmer
Hinkley, John, miller
Husher, James, jun. baker
Husher, James, carpenter and grocer
Kine, Joseph, farmer
Latter, Lawrence, farmer
Mabb, Alfred, shoemaker
Macdonald, John, draper and grocer
Martin, Thomas, farmer
Martin, William, relieving officer and registrar of births and deaths
Mercer, William, surgeon
Newington, Horace, shopkeeper
Newington, John Baker, farmer
Newington, Joseph Owen, watch and clock maker
Newington, Thomas, plumber
Noakes, William, tailor
Parrett, William, beer retailer and shoemaker
Pierson, Thomas, farmer
Pilbeam, Thomas and Richard, shoemakers
Pitt, Jacob, Greyhound inn
Playsted, Alfred, butcher
Playsted, George Luck, farmer

Playsted, Henry Alfred, farmer
Pope, Stephen, shopkeeper
Powell, Isaac, gunsmith
Reed, William, blacksmith
Rogers, Henry, carpenter
Rogers, John, farmer
Roger, William, shoemaker
Smith, George, farmer
Smith, Henry, currier
Smith, Jabez, postmaster, &c.
Smith, Joseph, jun. Railway tavern
Smith, Peter, currier
Smith, Samuel, carpenter
Smith, Thomas, farmer
Standen, John, farmer
Stevens, George, farmer and innkeeper, Hare and Hounds
Stollery, William, wheelwright
Swife, John, beer retailer
Swift, John, turner
Taylor, Miss Frances, Mark Cross
Till, Frederick, blacksmith and beer seller
Tompsett, Benjamin, farmer
Tompsett, James, farmer
Tompsett, John, jun. (executors to) farmer
Tompsett, John, jun. farmer
Tooth, Edward, Queen's Head and posting house
Vineall, John, farmer
Wait, Richard, saddler
Walker, William, horsedealer
Wallis and Ashby, stonemasons
Wallis, John, stonemason
Wenmam, John Gude, farmer
Wenmam, Thomas
Weston, Nathan, shopkeeper
Wickenden, John, farmer
Wicker, William, shopkeeper
Wright, William, shopkeeper

PRIVATE RESIDENTS.

Bruce —, South park
Clark William White
Cosserat Lewis, Prospect house
Daniel David, Cousley wood
De Murrieta Adrian & Christobel, Wadhurst park
Dixon Henry, J.P. Frankham
Foley Rev. John, B.D. [vicar], Vicarage
Gaston Francis G. Cousley wood
Gee Thomas, Dewhurst lodge
Groundwater Mrs. High house
Harland Henry
Jones Rev. James [Baptist]
Latter Lawrence, Sandy Den
Lowdell Surgeon-Major Charles, Bestbeech hill
Luck Frederick George, The Olives
McMahon Bernard, Wick
Mercer William
Newington Joseph John, Towngate
Playsted Alfred
Prideaux Walter, Faircrouch
Roberts Rev. Albert James, M.A. Tide Brook vicarage
Rogers Henry, Lower Church gate
Smyth Rt. Watson, J.P. Wadhurst castle
Thomas John F. T. Monks
Thompson Wm. Gordon, J.P. Mount ho
Till Thomas
Wace Rev. Richard Henry, M.A
Walker Capt. Wm. Fras. Buckhurst ldg

COMMERCIAL.

Adams Thomas, farmer, Darby
Allen James, grocer & draper
Apps William, turner
Ashby Charles, bricklayer
Ashby William, miller, River hall
Attwood William, beer retailer
Austen Henry Jeffery, auctioneer, appraiser, valuer, house, estate & land agent & farmer, Marling place
Austen John, farmer, White gate
Austen William (exors. of), farmer, Cousley wood
Avard George, farmer, Morgans
Avery George Wm. farmer, Great Pell
Bailey Edward, plumber &c
Baldock & Weekes, carpenters &c. Durgates
Baldwin John, carpenter
Baldwin Samuel, farmer
Ballard Ann (Miss), grocer, & post office, Cousley wood

Ballard John, *Old Vine inn*, Cousley wood
Ballard John, blacksmith
Barnham Nicholas, wheelwright
Barrow Joseph, farmer
Bassett Jas. wheelwright, Sparrow's grn
Benge Wm. Hy. grocer, Cousley wood
Bone James, shoe maker
Boorman Saml. saddler & harness maker
Boorman Thomas, farmer, Newnhams
Brissenden Charles, farmer
Brooks Joshua, baker
Bull Henry, registrar of births & deaths
Burt James, tailor
Butler Edward, farmer, Buttons
Carpenter Charles George, baker
Cheesman James, corn dealer & wool merchant & agent for C. S. Spence's shoddy manures
Collins John, *Red Lion*, Sparrow's green
Corke Obadiah Thomas, draper & grocer
Couchman Thomas, chemist, veterinary surgeon & farmer
Dadswell Edwin, hair dresser
Davis David, bricklayer
Fairbrother Horace & Saml. brick makers
Fuggles Misses, ladies' school, New house
Gallup George, blacksmith
Gibb David William, wheelwright, Bestbeech hill
Hallett John, farmer, Church settle
Hammond Albert, farmer, Muddle farm
Hammond Edwd. cooper, Sparrow's grn
Hammond Edwd. *White Hart*, & butcher
Harland Henry, surgeon
Harmer James, farmer
Head Edward, beer retailer, Tide brook
Hemsley George, basket maker
Hemsley Wm. blacksmith, Sparrow's grn
Humphrey James, farmer, Lodge hill
Husher Thomas, carpenter
Kemp George, beer retailer, Stream
Kine Edward Joseph, farmer
Latter Lawrence, hop factor, Sandy Den
Luck George, plumber, Durgates
Mabb Alfred, shoe maker
Macdonald Maria (Miss), draper & grocer
Markwick George, grocer, Durgates
Mercer William, surgeon
Mott Mary (Mrs.), straw bonnet maker
Neaves Thomas, *Hare & Hounds*, Best beech hill
Newington Horace, shopkeeper, Sparrow's green
Newington Horace, watch & clock maker

Newington John Baker, farmer, Foxholes
Newington Joseph John, farmer & landowner, Towngate
Pierson Thomas, farmer
Pilbeam Edward, boot & shoe maker
Pilbeam Richard, boot & shoe maker
Pilbeam Thomas, boot & shoe maker
Pitt Jacob, *Greyhound*, & assistant overseer & collector
Pope Stephen, shopkeeper
Rabson Joseph, farmer, Bassetts
Reed William, blacksmith
Rose Thomas, farmer, Buckland hill
Smith Geo. (exors. of), farmer, Newhouse
Smith Henry, currier
Smith Jabez, postmaster
Smith James, farmer
Smith John, farmer, Durgates
Smith Joseph, *Railway hotel commercial & posting house*, quarry owner & brick & tile maker, coal merchant, & agent for Rickman & Co.'s lime & guano, Railway station
Smith Peter, currier, Tidebrook
Smith Rowland, butcher
Standen John, miller, Cousley wood
Stollory William, wheelwright
Styles James, grocer & carrier
Thompsett Charity (Mrs.), farmer, Earl's farm
Tompsett Jas. & Dennis, farmers, Wenbans
Tompsett John, farmer, Crouches
Tompsett John, farmer, Scragoak
Tooth Edward, farmer & coal merchant
Tribe Charles, shopkeeper & carrier, Bestbeech hill
Usherwood Barnes, farmer, Cliff Buttons
Wait Elizabeth (Miss), day school
Walker William, farmer & horse dealer, Ash grove
Wallis George, bricklayer & stonemason
Wenman John Gude, farmer, Great Shoesmith
White George, miller
White Richard, relieving officer
Wickenden John, farmer, Lucks
Williams Robert, *Queen's Head*
Williams Thomas, farmer, Wickhurst
Wood Elizabeth Ann (Miss), berlin wool repository
Wright Gregory, brewer of genuine home brewed ales & porter, Holmesdale brewery
Wright Gregory, *Castle inn*, & fly proprietor

37

High Street in the 1890s - notice the iron pentices. Furthermost left can be seen people standing outside the original White Hart pub

In 1901 many inhabitants are coming in from outside to the area. Is the railway becoming more popular? The families moving in are workers. A blacksmith, Joseph Home, arrives from Dorset; a draper's assistant, Tom Tucker and family, move in from Somerset; a Essex father, William Carter - from Woodham Ferris, is a carter, and a farming family, Morley Browne with his wife and four children, arrives from Cambridgeshire.

SOURCES

Census returns 1841 - 1901

Christopher Bell: *East Sussex County Council, 1889-1974,* Phillimore 1975

ESRO

Harry and Horace Newington at the Clock House in 1900

Post Office and telegraph boys

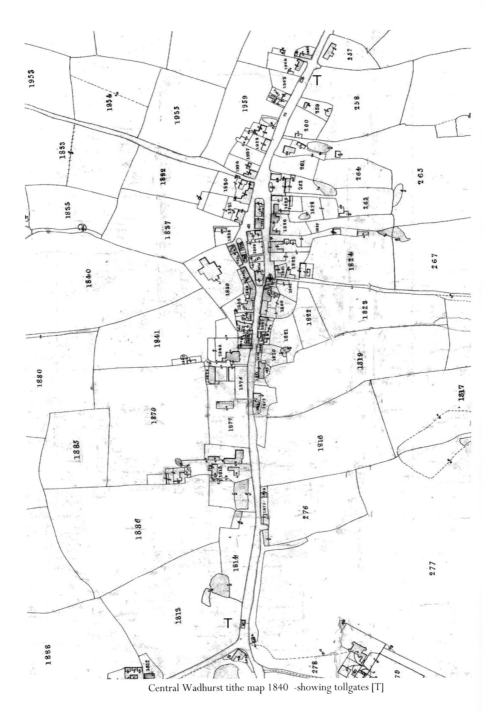

Central Wadhurst tithe map 1840 -showing tollgates [T]

THE TURNPIKE AND TOLLGATES
RACHEL RING

Turnpike: defensive frame of pikes, gate set across road to stop carts etc until toll is paid

Tollgate: bar or usually gate across road to prevent passage

Tollhouse: house built to home tollgate keeper usually alongside tollgate

Turnpike road: road with a gate or barrier preventing access. Common from the mid 16th-19th century

Turnpike Trust: appointed trustees to administer local turnpike

The upkeep of roads in medieval times fell to the landowner but in Tudor times legislation put the responsibility in the hands of the Parish with every householder having to contribute six days' work a year.

In around 1663 an early turnpike trust was formed to administer the collection of tolls for repair of a road between Wadesmill in Hertfordshire and Stilton in Huntingdonshire.

During the 18th and mid 19th century many other such trusts were formed and each needed an Act of Parliament before it could operate. Over a thousand such trusts were set up administering at least 23,000 miles of road.

Unfortunately many trusts were fraudulently administered and in 1820 a further Act of Parliament required trusts to keep annual accounts which were submitted to the Secretary of State.

By the mid 19th century the competition from the railways, and heavier road traffic, meant the trusts were unable to cope. Their long held administration problems and the lack of funds (many had huge debts) caused Parliament to withdraw their powers so during the 1860/70s most were wound up, the last trust being so done in 1895.

When a road became dis-turnpiked in this way it became an ordinary highway and its maintenance was the responsibility of the local inhabitants but the long term responsibility fell upon the local authority through whose district it passed. This was seen as unfair and the Highways and Locomotive (Amendment) Act was passed making all dis-turnpiked roads after 1870 main roads. Half of the maintenance was to be paid by Quarter Sessions to the Local Highway Authorities who maintained them. This too was unsatisfactory and the Local Government Act of 1888 put the whole burden of maintenance of most roads on the new County Councils.

Looking specifically now at Sussex, (ESRO QDJ/EW1) by 1820, the year an Act required accounts to be prepared, we read that turnpiked roads covered some 521 miles of the county. The statement continues:

Amount of Income	£32,252.0.0.
Income debts	£180,450.0.0.
Annual Expenditure	£28,384.0.0.
Annual Interest due	£43,000.0.0.

The earliest gated road was in 1710, Sevenoaks to Tunbridge Wells (ending just into Sussex) and the last one in 1841 Cripps Corner to Hawkhurst.

With the cessation of the trusts, gates were demolished; the vast majority of the tollhouses were also demolished, often due to their close proximity to the road and the need for wider highways.

Toll-gate and cottage from Beeding - for comparative purposes
[now in the Weald and Downland Museum, Singleton]

During the research into the design of tollhouses it was found that each area erected its own style of property using local materials. Certainly in Sussex our tollhouses followed a very simple single storey design. They were humble, two roomed, weather-boarded houses with a bedroom and a living room cum kitchen. An example one can view internally is at the Weald and Downland Open Air Museum at Singleton.

However, Wadhurst still has one at the top of Tapsells Lane, now a private extended home. Another superb example is on the corner of Cross Lane at Ticehurst. Photographs exist of one on the triangle of grass on the road in front of Ladymeads in Lower Cousley Wood still showing a weather-boarded frontage.

Paygate Cottage in the Lower High Street around the turn of the century

The research area we followed took the tollgate outside the Primary School and diagonally opposite the entrance to the Castle, down to the Lower High Street toll. No evidence was found of a tollhouse by the Castle although ancient maps clearly showed a gate there. Could the keeper have lived in the house at the top of Tapsells Lane we wonder?

The gate in the Lower High Street is clearly shown on the Courthope map and on OS ones around 1840 by the entrance to Walters Cottages. Census returns of that time list the tollgate keeper as residing somewhere near where

Tollgate Cottage - Ticehurst

the Youth Centre now is. Then a decade later a small house is shown on the eastern side of Laurel Bank and was known locally as Paygate Cottage. The only photograph we have seen of this "tollhouse" is more contemporary and does not show it to be weather-boarded but given all the others in and around Wadhurst we have no reason to believe that it would not have been of the same construction. Also it is conceivable that this property was built before the maps we studied showed evidence of it. Sadly, Wadhurst has retained virtually no documents of this important era of highway history.

Milestones were voluntarily erected at first but compulsorily so by an Act of Parliament in 1766. From what we ascertained these stones are being recorded and preserved as another important part of highway history. So many were removed, and subsequently lost, during the war and others in road-widening schemes. Wadhurst is fortunate still to have one at the site of the Castle tollgate.

Another relic of relevance to mapping and measuring is the Ordnance Survey height marker post [*right*] in the Lower High Street.

The ESRO document QDT/EW1 offered almost the only information on the Mayfield and Wadhurst Turnpike Trust. Each page was headed "1 Geo 4 ch 95" - the first year of George 4 reign Chapter 95". It referred to the 1820 Act whereby all trustees had to prepare accounts to be submitted by 1st September and that the Clerk of the Peace was also required by 1st October to transmit all such returns to the Office of His Majesty's Principal Secretary of State for the Home Department.

This document went on to say that any wilful omission by any clerk or treasurer for each offence would pay £50 to His Majesty's Courts of Record at Westminster.

The Clerk of the Peace was instructed that "all Returns be fairly and accurately copied and kept in books in office of the Clerk of the Peace, who can allow any person to inspect the copies by paying an Inspection Sum of two shillings". To acquire a copy would cost five shillings.

For undertaking this, the Clerk of the Peace received for every return copied into such a book and the original sent to the Secretary of State, two guineas. There was a further five shillings payable for other services mentioned in the Act.

A further instruction to turnpike trustees in this Act was that they should be appointed subject to a property qualification and in turn were empowered to appoint a clerk, treasurer, surveyor and toll collector. Loans were raised to provide for the building of tollhouses and the erection of tollgates, and the securities given were mortgages on the tolls.

The Act required answers to ten questions and the large, scripted documents were sent to both the clerk and treasurer of each trust to be completed individually. We were fortunate to find that we could view two returns made from Wadhurst with the handwriting of the clerk and the treasurer on each - should these have been forwarded to the Secretary of State we wonder? The only other returns in the book were the Clerk of the Peace's copies.

One question asked the length of the road and its precise location: answer, "Wadhurst District of the road extending from Sleechers Cross in the Parish of Frant to Swiftsden in the Parish of Etchingham. 10 Miles and 14 rods".

Another answer given was the "principal debt on security by mortgage of the tolls £2470.0s.0d. excluding the sum of £25 supposed to have been relinquished, floating debt about £54".

The Annual Income shown was £573.15s.3d.

The amount of expenditure was £617.15s.4d. Further questions asked for details of the balance due to the Treasurer at the last Settlement: answer, £31.8s.11d. Was any interest due and unpaid: answer, £30.9s.6d. exclusive of interest on the supposed relinquished debt of £25.

Whether any and what Sinking Fund had been established, and if so what amount of debt it has liquidated: answer, "There is no Sinking Fund Established".

The final question asked for "dates and chapters of the several Acts of Parliament from which the Trustees derive their authority".

Answer,	7th	Geo 3	ca 84
	12th	do	ca 92
	48th	do	ca 68

This confirms the information on Armstrong's map over the page that the Mayfield and Wadhurst Turnpike Trust was first granted permission to operate

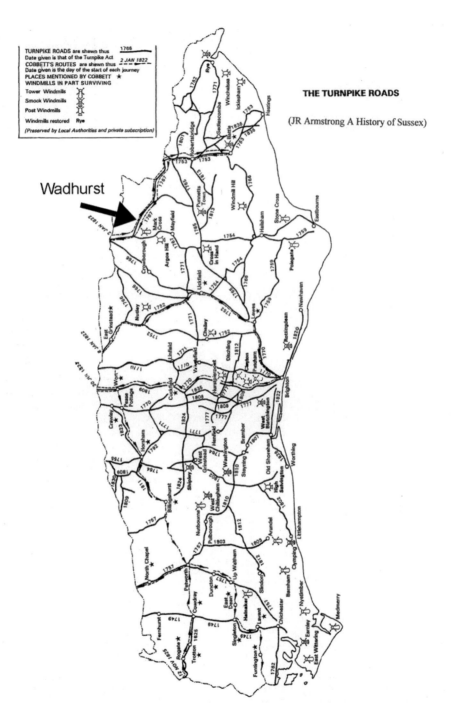

THE TURNPIKE ROADS

(JR Armstrong A History of Sussex)

Wadhurst

TURNPIKE ROADS are shewn thus
Date given is that of the Turnpike Act
COBBETT'S ROUTES are shewn thus
Date given is the day of the start of each journey
PLACES MENTIONED BY COBBETT ★
WINDMILLS IN PART SURVIVING

Tower Windmills
Smock Windmills
Post Windmills
Windmills restored   Rye
(Preserved by Local Authorities and private subscription)

in 1767 (the 7th year of the reign of George III); the other dates above would be 1772 and 1808 respectively.

Then followed the formal signing and witnessing of the document as follows:-

"I do sware that this return and all things therein contained is and are true to the best of my knowledge and belief and that I have not wilfully omitted anything required to be returned by me. So help me God."

It was signed by H Playsted, Treasurer.

* "if the party making the Return is a Quaker then by Affirmation to the same effect" *

Beneath this followed:-

"I do certify that the above Return was signed and verified upon oath before me"

It was then initialled by the Justice of the Peace for the County of Sussex.

The very same questions were put to the Clerk, R Haley (?); the signature of the clerk was difficult to decipher.

It was disappointing that, despite our research into the background of turnpike trusts, and the 1820 returns called for by Act of Parliament, there is a substantial lack of further detail about the Wadhurst tollgates, apart from a comment in the Church Vestry records of 15th March 1856 that the trustees of the turnpike be asked if there are monies which they have in their power to expend on road repairs, and the following information from the census returns:

				Age		Inferred
1841						
Wadhurst Town	WAITE	William		24	Tollgate Keeper	Lower
Town	MARYON	John		60	Tollgate Keeper	Upper
1851						
Toll House	CORNWELL	James	Head	39	Toll Gate Keeper	Upper
Toll House	CORNWELL	Sarah	Wife	44		
1861						
Village	GREEN	John	Head	66	Tollgate Keeper	Lower
Village	GREEN	Annabella	Wife	63		
Toll Gate Cottage	BODY	John		40	Toll Collector	Upper?
1871						
Village	BELLINGHAM	June	Head	41	Toll Gate Keeper	Upper
Village	BELLINGHAM	Horace	Son	11	Scholar	
Village	BELLINGHAM	Daniel	Son	7	Scholar	
Toll Gate House	JENNER	John	Head	73	Ag Lab	Pell Green
Toll Gate House	JENNER	Miriam	Wife	69	Toll collector	
Toll Gate House	JENNER	Rhoda	Daur	29	Domestic servant	

This evidence is somewhat confusing. The above is a list of all those who are described as toll gate keeper or collector. There are also entries in 1851 for James Maryan shoe maker master and his family at the Toll House in the Lower High Street but there is no indication that they operated the toll gate. The entries do, however, show that tolls were still being collected in Wadhurst in 1871; indeed the 1878 OS map still shows a gate across the Lower High Street: ongoing research may reveal further information.

Another research topic could be the provision of piped water to Wadhurst - we have evidence in St James's Square of the Crowborough and District Water Company to start from.

SOURCES

ESRO
Internet Tollhouses and Milestones
Tithe Map 1840
Weald and Downland Museum Guide
Armstrong J R A History of Sussex

STREET LIGHTING

RACHEL RING

This interesting report, prepared by the Committee of Wadhurst Street Lighting for their 7th AGM in April 1894, started another search for us into the background of illumination.

WADHURST STREET LIGHTING.

COMMITTEE :
MR. F. AUSTEN, Chairman.

DR. WHITE, Hon. Collector.   MR. O. T. CORKE, Treasurer.

MR. G. TULLEY.   MR. R. SMITH.   MR. W. H. NEWINGTON.   MR. C. W. ASHBY.

MR. F. W. LARCOMBE, Secretary.

— Seventh Annual Report, —
ENDING APRIL, 1894.

TO THE SUBSCRIBERS AND PARISHIONERS,

In presenting the Annual Report of the Street Lighting, the Committee regret that it was not so entirely satisfactory as they could wish, this was owing to the illness of the lamplighter, when no efficient substitute could be found. The Committee hope to remedy this in the future.

They again regret having to curtail somewhat the Lighting Season, owing to a balance due to the Treasurer ; but this they consider might be easily remedied if those of the Wadhurst Trade who do not at present subscribe, would contribute their proportionate share towards the expenses, considering the benefit they undoubtedly receive from the light thrown on their premises. Should the contributions continue to decrease or prove insufficient for the purpose, the Committee will be compelled to apply, through the Vestry, for power to enforce a rate for the proper maintenance of the Lighting (See Act of Parliament for the Lighting of Parishes, William IV. Cap. 90.)

To reduce the Working Expenses, Dr. White has kindly consented to act as Honorary Collector ; it is therefore hoped that the Subscriptions—NOW DUE—will be sent to him as early as possible, or paid on the first application.

FRANK AUSTEN, CHAIRMAN.
O. T. CORKE, TREASURER.
F. W. LARCOMBE, SECRETARY.

From the statement to "the Subscribers and Parishioners" we can ascertain that lighting of sorts was introduced to the High Street in 1887 but what was its source - oil or gas?

At ESRO the only reference to lighting that could be found was relating to a document lodged on 29th November 1901 for "Incorporation to supply Gas to Wadhurst and other parishes...... to supply gas for lighting, heating etc.". Act of Parliament 1901 - Session 1902, Wadhurst Gas.

The short printed document dated 8th November 1901 was prepared, and lodged some three weeks later, by Baker Lees and Co., 54 Parliament Street, Westminster, solicitors and Parliamentary Agents.

So, we see that whilst officially records show 1901 as the year of introduction, the Act of Parliament session fell in 1902 when permission was granted.

Accompanying maps showed the land on which gasometers were to be built. Two sites were applied for, one at Wadhurst and one at Ticehurst. The Wadhurst property was described as:- "Field and rough owned by Henry Tarleton Whitty and occupied by John George Selby" (farmer); a similar field was also in the proposal. The site was diagonally across the road from Greenman Farm and next to Dewhurst Cottages.

Dewhurst Cottages and Gasworks

The Ticehurst description of property read:- "Wood, owned by George John Courthope and occupied by George James Badcock" and the second area was "field and occupation road" again owned by George Courthope but shown as "In Hand". As far as the map led us, this site was opposite Witherenden Mill but we have no evidence that this site was actually used.

What this research told us was that the 7th AGM Notice of Wadhurst Street Lighting must have referred to oil lit lamps since gas powered lighting was still about seven or eight years away.

To date our research has not enabled us to identify under whose auspices the Wadhurst Street Lighting Committee was managed but we assume it to have been the Parish Council.

VICTORIAN ONE STOP AND WOOD-B-PINE

DAVID JAMES

On 28th July 1817 Samuel Baldwin, innkeeper, purchased properties from Edward Paige of Wadhurst, butcher, and heir of John Elliott "late of Wadhurst, carpenter, deceased". It is recorded in a series of documents which are held by the Wadhurst History Society (Reference 05/AM/001) and which indicate the history of the High Street properties in the 18th and 19th Centuries. Samuel's acquisition was "in the fifty seventh year of the reign of our sovereign Lord George the Third."

Meanwhile, far beyond Wadhurst, George III's age did not escape the thoughts of Edward, Duke of Kent. Although only the fourth son of George he was aware that his elder brothers were all over fifty and that, as Christopher Hibbert observed in his *History of Queen Victoria,* while "George III had no fewer than fifty six grand children none was legitimate". The Duke of Kent had an eye on his posterity. He arranged for the return of his mistress, Julie de St. Laurent, to Paris and made overtures for the hand of Victoire of Saxe-Coburg-Saarfeld. They married in May 1818. Within a year the future Queen Victoria was born and in January 1820 the Duke of Kent preceded his unbalanced father to the grave.

Samuel Baldwin had paid £275 for "all that messuage [*a dwelling house and its adjacent buildings and the adjacent land used by the household]* and tenement now in two dwellings together with the new....... Shops and outbuildings, yard and garden thereto belonging and now occupied by Mr. William Baldwin and Miss Blunden, spinster." A subsequent document in 1829 "in the tenth year of the reign of our Sovereign Lord George the Fourth" shows Samuel securing a mortgage from Thomas Piper of Mayfield, plumber and glazier, on the property for two hundred and twenty three pounds and ten shillings at 5% annual interest. William Noakes, who is described as a draper and grocer, acted as Trustee for Samuel.

The 1840 Tithe Map [over] helps to locate the properties. As well as being George Courthope's tenant at The Greyhound, Samuel Baldwin is shown as owning two properties near the Queen's Head. The smaller property, number

1863 on the map, was on the corner of Washwell Lane, and measured three perches, some ninety square metres. Two other smaller properties separated it from the Queen's Head [1866], which was also opposite a house belonging to William Noakes.

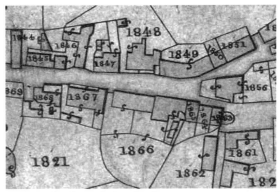

The 1829 mortgage deed confirms the location, mentioning that it adjoined "the lands late of Mr Henry Playsted and now of Mr Alfred Playsted on the south." The Tithe Map shows Alfred owning property number 1862 immediately to the south of 1863, as well as his more substantial property in the High Street itself. Samuel Baldwin's eastern property [1863 and below] now provides the foundation of part of what is now One Stop, and his larger one, 1867 on the Tithe map, was located on what is now the forecourt of Wood-B-Pine.

Looking up the High Street from Washwell Lane - the tea rooms on the left are one of the properties mentioned in the Deeds

Samuel and his colleagues would all have been delighted to hear news of the seventeen year old Princess Victoria's visit to their area in the autumn of 1834. Her Journal describes her enjoyment of Tunbridge Wells and her rides in the surrounding countryside, and how she left "dear" Tunbridge Wells for St. Leonards and Hastings on 4th November with "GREAT REGRET". She found her visit to the Weald to be a much greater pleasure than her visit as Queen to East Sussex in 1845. Her Journal describes how in Brighton "We were mobbed by all the shopboys in the town who ran and looked under my bonnet." This encouraged her to seek the seclusion of Osborne House on the Isle of Wight the following year.

The stables of the old Queen's Head and the adjacent building, no.1867 owned by Samuel Baldwin and now the forecourt of Wood-B-Pine

Rising house prices are not just a modern phenomenon. The £275 which Samuel Baldwin paid in 1817 brought a significant profit to Edward Paige who had bought the property for £170 in 1801 from John Martin, a carpenter. Edward had also ensured that John provided a bond for £100 lest "Constant (now wife of the said John Martin) may have or challenge to have her Dower or Thirds in case she shall happen to survive the said John Martin her husband."

John himself had made a profit on the properties, although there may have been developments, since the contract of 1801 provides the first reference to there being shops as well as dwellings. He had paid £65 to Ann Mabb for them in October 1780. Hers was a fairly simple property, contrasting with the little under £7000 which the Prime Minister, William Pitt the Younger, paid for Holwood House near Bromley just five years later - a house which his sister

Harriet described as only "a small House which will not allow of many visitors", consisting of six bedrooms and two hundred acres.

The properties in Wadhurst, however, clearly indicated a trend of rising inflation. The price of £65 in 1780 became £700 eighty-six years later when John Wooden and his sister Susannah secured what the notice of sale described as the "valuable commercial freehold property at auction at The Queen's Head Inn, Wadhurst at 4 for 5 o'clock precisely on Tuesday, September 25th, 1866."

The bill of sale describes how the premises comprised "two double fronted shops, with counting house, commanding warehouses behind, Parlour, Kitchen. Cellar, Two Show Rooms and one attic, and an adjoining private house counting five bedrooms, one attic, one sitting room, yard and stabling." The premises were "let on a lease for a term of 7 years from Midsummer 1866" to Mr. Hope, Grocer and Draper at a rental of £65 per annum."

At this time the property's ownership was changing hands as often as the occupants of 10, Downing Street, since the years 1865-1868 saw four Prime Ministers, Earl Russell, the Earl of Derby, Disraeli and Gladstone, and the property had a similar number of owners. Victoria herself was having a stressful time. Her Journal entry for 15th March 1861 had expressed "Oh, what agony, what despair, was this," as she comforted her dying mother. Worse followed. Before the end of that year the Royal Archives for 11th December describe how Victoria "dropped on my knees in mute and distracted despair, unable to utter a word or shed a tear" as she entered the room where her husband, the Prince Consort, lay dying.

Queen Victoria's mourning continued for years and a similar gloom was evident in the Wadhurst High Street properties. In the mid 1860's solicitors' enquiries after the 1866 auction (Cole and Mortgagees to Wooden, 1st December 1866) show that the property had been owned by Charles Harris. The 1861 census shows him living there as a grocer and draper who had been born in Pluckley, along with his wife Eliza, formerly of Frant, who at twenty-six was two years older than him. They had no children but a fourteen year old apprentice and a sixteen year old servant.

The problems developed after Charles sold the property to William Selby Cole. The 1866 solicitors' enquiries refer to a conveyance of 13th October 1865 being the conveyance to Cole and state that "Cole is a young man certainly not 40 years of age". William's new project did not prosper. A deed of 25th August 1866 from Mr. William Selby Cole to Messrs. H. and W. Mumford is actually a "Conveyance for the benefit of Creditors". He was bankrupt. The Mumfords were warehousemen of 36, Bread Street, London. Selby Cole was conveying "all his estates and effects" to his creditors. Hence the auction the following month.

WADHURST, SUSSEX.

VALUABLE FREEHOLD INVESTMENT.

PARTICULARS AND CONDITIONS OF SALE

OF A

Valuable Commercial Freehold Property,

SITUATE ON THE

South Side of the Main Street in Wadhurst, in the County of Sussex,

And in the occupation of Mr. HOPE, Grocer and Draper.

For Absolute Sale

By direction of Trustees, under Deed of Assignment, with consent of the Mortgagee.

BY

COOK, IZARD & SMITH

AT

THE "QUEEN'S HEAD INN,"

WADHURST,

ON TUESDAY, SEPTEMBER 25th, 1866,

At 4 for 5 o'clock precisely.

The Premises Comprise:—Two Double Fronted Shops, with Counting House commanding Warehouses behind, Parlor, Kitchen, Cellar, Two Show Rooms, and One Attic, on First Floor.

The Private House which adjoins contains Five Bed Rooms, One Attic, and One Sitting Room; Yard and Stabling.

Let on a Lease for a term of 7 years from Midsummer, 1866, at a Rental of

£65 PER ANNUM.

The Property may be viewed by permission of Mr. HOPE, the Tenant; Particulars and Conditions of Sale may be had at the place of Sale; of Mr. HOPE, on the Premises; of G. HINDS, Esq., Solicitor, Goudhurst; Messrs. LANFEAR & STEWART, Solicitors, Abchurch Lane, E.C.; Messrs. LADBURY, COLLINSON, & VINEY, Public Accountants, 99, Cheapside; and of the

AUCTIONEERS, 45, CHEAPSIDE, LONDON, E.C.

MERRITT & HATCHER, Printers, 2, Grocers' Hall Court, Poultry, E.C.

Nor was there a happy resolution when John James Wooden's bid was successful. A deed of 4th February 1867 by Bolton, Robbins and Buck of Lincolns Inn Fields gives "short particulars of the property at Wadhurst". It is headed "In Lunacy", describes John as a "person of unsound mind", and suggests that the interests of the Mumfords had not yet been resolved.

There is no indication of the Woodens living in the High Street in any of the censuses 1871-1901, but their ownership continued. A mortgage deed of 25th February 1895 shows John still "a person of unsound mind" and a committee acting on his behalf to arrange a loan of £150, extended by a further £50 at 5% interest from Spencer Smith of Middlesex. John was reliable in meeting his obligations, since a mortgage transfer of 3rd February 1906 on Spencer Smith's death showed that while the capital was still outstanding "all interest thereon had been paid up."

The Woodens may not have lived there themselves, but others did. The 1895 mortgage, a little short of Christian names, refers to the "said messuage and tenement formerly in two dwellings but now in four dwellings together with four shops and building yards gardens coachhouses and stables thereto belonging....now in the occupation of ....Foord.....Wright....Ruth Martin....Farmer and .....Newington."

The 1891 census mentions three of these households. As well as lots of Newingtons it refers to Ruth Martin. She was a 64 year old widow and caretaker, living with her 34 year old daughter, Sarah, a dressmaker, and Owen her 26 year old carpenter son. Next door to them was the family of Willis Foord, a boot and shoemaker.

They had all enjoyed the celebrations marking Queen Victoria's Golden Jubilee in 1887, perhaps more so than her grandson Prince Wilhelm, who was not quite yet Kaiser Wilhelm II. John Rohl's study of Wilhelm's early life shows him to be even more outspoken than usual during his visit to London. He commented that it was "high time the old woman died....She causes trouble more than one would think. Well, England should look out when I have something to say about things....One cannot have enough hatred for England". The next generation in Wadhurst High Street would be sending soldiers to the Western Front and Aubers Ridge.

Meanwhile Wooden may have been brooding over his legal fees which he had paid on 1st March 1867 for the conveyance of his property. The carefully written account, detailing 33 items, amounted to £25-7s-8d. Lest current property owners consider such an amount wistfully it totalled some four per cent of the purchase price.

It had all begun one hundred and thirty years earlier. Probate had been granted on 21st March 1739 on the last will and testament which John Mercer, cooper, had prepared four years earlier. It opened as a good Christian's will

Mr Wooden

Attending Mr Smith on his handing me Abstract and Contract and taking instructions to peruse abstract ————	6 - 8
Perusing and Considering Abstract (24 Sheets)	2 - 13 - 4
Drawing requisition upon Title ————	13 - 4
Instructions to Mr Cory to peruse Abstract of Title and settle requisitions	6 - 8
Attending him therewith and for same	6 - 8
Paid his fee & Clerk (see below	
Copy requisitions as settled by him for Vendors Solicitors ————	6 - 8
Attending them with same ————	6 - 8
Perusing and considering replies thereto	6 - 8
Attending you reading over replies & conferring and when you consented to waive some of the requisitions ———	6 - 8
Writing Vendors Solicitor thereon —	3 - 6
Writing Vendors Solicitor appointing time to examine Deeds ————	3 - 6
Attending examining Deeds with Abstract ————	13 - 4
Attending Registry of Trust Deeds in Bankruptcy searching for and inspecting Deed executed by Mr Cole	6 - 8
Paid (see below) ————	
Attending Common Pleas Registry searching Judgment &c ————	13 - 4
Paid (see below ————	
Instructions for Conveyance —	6 - 8
	8 - 0 - 4

57

should: "In the name of God Amen.... I commend my soul into the hands of Almighty God, trusting my Lord and Saviour Jesus Christ to have full pardon of all my sins. My Body I commend to the earth to be buryed in such Christian like manner as my ....heirs shall think fitt. And as for the disposition of such temporal estate as it hath pleased God to bestow upon me, I give and dispose of these as follows."

John then defined a range of kinsfolk from a variety of trades - cooper, carpenter, upholsterer - each of whom was to receive £5. He appointed "my loving friend and neighbour Edward Burgis of Wadhurst" to administer the will, for which he was to receive "one and twenty shillings over and above all charges which he shall sustain."

However, he gave the bulk of his estate "to Ann Wickham, spinster, one of the daughters of my brother in law Richard Wickham of Wadhurst, shoemaker, who now liveth with me and keepeth my house. In regard of her tender care and faithful service to me and my late wife, all that messuage or tenement, garden and bankside situate and being at or near Wadhurst town, which I heretofore purchased of Mr. Thomas Shorte deceased, now in my own occupation.... And all residue to Ann."

Ann was later to marry and to become Ann Mabb, selling the property in 1780. In the meantime she enjoyed the benefits which were the reward of her kindness to John Mercer, and which were to become the basis of some of the trade in the High Street during the reign of Queen Victoria.

FROM WADHURST TO RED DEER
OLIVE MAUDE LUCK AND ALBERT ERNEST ROBERTS
EMMA RICHARDSON

As you enter the Parish Church of St Peter and St Paul you will see on your left a large stained glass window. The wording on this window is

'In loving memory of Olive Maude Roberts 2nd August 1899'.

Olive was born in Wadhurst on the 11th of October 1876. She was the seventh of nine surviving children and the youngest daughter of Frederick and Fanny Luck of The Olives, Churchsettle Lane.

Frederick George Luck, a timber merchant, and Fanny Elizabeth Walker were married in Edmonton in 1867. Fanny was the sister of the famous sporting Walker Brothers who played cricket for Middlesex County Cricket Club during the second half of the 19th century. Her Brother Isaac Donnithorne Walker was captain of the team for some time and the family had donated a field for the original team to play on.

Their first two children were born in East Barnet, Frederick Charles in 1868 and his sister Caroline in 1869. The family moved after this to Wadhurst. More children followed in quick succession, Fanny Louisa in 1870, Edith in 1872, Norah in 1873, twins Annie and Susie in 1874, Olive Maude in the autumn of 1876 and finally Oliver in 1883.

The family were at The Olives by 1871 where they had employed head nurse Mrs Isabel Roberts from Wales, a cook, 27 year old Ann Wain, a parlour maid named Sarah Rince, a house maid Mary Ann Barton from nearby Robertsbridge and a nurse maid 16 year old Mary Matthews who was probably doing most of the caring for 8 month old Fanny Louisa as well as the other two children.

The girls were educated at home and in 1881 their governess and teacher was Mina Horn, a 21 year old German girl. By 1881 Frederick Jnr had left the family home and was being educated in Brenchley at Matfield Grange Vicarage and Private School for Boys where he was one of 31 boys from all over the world being tutored by George Plume.

The family seemed to be very much part of village life. The girls took a great deal of interest in the schooling of the village children and visited the school room often to watch the children work and also listen to them sing.

While Olive was growing up in the village, her future husband was residing a couple of miles away at Tidebrook Vicarage.

Born on the 12th of March 1870 in Tidebrook Albert Ernest was the sixth of ten children born to Albert James Roberts and his wife Ellen. Albert Roberts Snr was the Vicar of Tidebrook and baptised all his children. The church had been completed in 1858 and according to the Sussex edition of the Post Office Directory 1859 Albert Roberts Snr was the incumbent at that time. In 1861 he was unmarried.

Albert's mother Ellen died in 1880 leaving 8 children at home ranging from 17 to two years. Besides the children there were three adults, her husband Reverend Roberts and his unmarried siblings Selina aged 55 and Charles aged 60. There were four live-in members of staff. The eldest son Charles (15) was at Marlborough College in Wiltshire and his brother Alfred (13) was with him.

The role of substitute mother probably fell somewhat on the shoulders of 17 year old Mary Eulielia. In May 1886 she placed the following advert in The Sussex Express:

"Wanted in a clergyman's family a good plain cook. A small dairy. Assistance given in the kitchen. A boy kept to clean knives. £20 a year all round, washing put out - Miss Roberts, Tidebrook Vicarage, Wadhurst, Hawkhurst."

Throughout my research I found many mentions of the vicar and his daughters visiting Tidebrook School. They gave out many of the prizes awarded to the youngsters for good attendance and for passing exams. The vicar often took news to the school from the Education Board as well.

In 1889 there was a meeting held in the Village which was reported in the local paper:

Tunbridge Wells Gazette Friday 5th March 1889

Wadhurst - Emigration

'Yesterday (Thursday) evening at the school room a meeting was held, when a lecture was given on "emigration to Canada and English colonies". One of the committee and the secretary from the self help emigration society attended and gave information of the society's operations.'

Many people were leaving England at this time for Canada. Help was available for the poor who wished to try for a better life in a new country, and ships were frequent, leaving from Liverpool, Bristol, Plymouth and Southampton.

It seems that it wasn't only the poor who looked for a new life in foreign lands. For a family with a fixed income of £200 to £400 a comfortable lifestyle was to be had in Canada. Albert was bitten by the bug and by the early 1890's seems to have left England heading for Canada.

He probably sailed from Liverpool to Quebec, Canada - a journey which would have taken around 2 or 3 weeks in a steamer. Fares in those days from Liverpool to Quebec would have been around $40 or $50 for a passage in Saloon Class including meals.

On the census of 5th of April 1891 his widowed father and all of his siblings (Charles, Mary, Alfred, Ellen, Lucy, Ethel, George, Frederick and 12 year old Edmund) are staying at Haworth Castle in Yorkshire where they are the guests of the Earl and Countess of Carlisle - Charles and Rosalind Howard. The special occasion was the forthcoming marriage, which took place 2 days later, of Lady Cecilia Howard and Charles Henry Roberts, Albert's brother. Albert had probably left the country by then as he was the only sibling not to attend the wedding. Also at the castle was one Maurice Llewelyn Davies who Albert's eldest sister, Mary Eulielia, was to marry later that spring in Wadhurst. Davies was a Manager working for Alfred Holt & Co of Liverpool, which was a steamship company. Perhaps Maurice made Albert's travel arrangements as he seems to have known the family well at the time but I have been unable to locate the ship that Albert sailed on.

In November 1894 Albert purchased just over 260 acres of land from the Canadian Pacific Railway close to the settlement of Red Deer in Alberta. He paid $3.00 an acre for the land at Red Deer River Valley, which was a good place for grain growing, dairy farming and ranching.

Prior to European settlement, the area that Albert choose to start his new life was inhabited by several different tribes and later by fur traders. Red Deer was a tiny area next to the Red Deer River after which the town was named. It lay mid way between Calgary and Edmonton in Alberta. The population was 128 people at the time of Albert Roberts' arrival and it was little more than a settlement with a trading post which had opened in 1883 to trade with Europe. With the completion of the Canadian Pacific Railway also in 1883 and then a stagecoach service between Calgary and Edmonton transport improved for the area and brought many more settlers. By November 1890, the Calgary-Red Deer line of the Calgary and Edmonton Railroad was complete. It became a town in 1901 with a population of 343. Today the population is about 75,000.

61

Albert became a rancher, or a homesteader. A homestead was an area of 160 acres usually with a farm house. He probably raised horses or cattle, although the land was also extremely good for growing crops.

After 2 or 3 years of building up his new home Albert returned to England to find a bride to take back to Canada. He returned to Wadhurst and married Miss Olive Maude Luck. Olive would have only been 14 or 15 when Albert had emigrated so it is unlikely that any marriage arrangements would have been made prior to him leaving.

From Wadhurst Parish Register—7th July 1898

Albert Ernest Roberts, 28, bachelor, Gent of Tidebrook and son of Albert J Roberts (Clerk in holy orders) and Olive Maude Luck, 21, spinster of Wadhurst, daughter of Frederick George Luck (deceased). Married by Banns by me W May Vicar of Brenchley witnessed by Ernest J Luck Norah M Luck Edith Luck

Sussex Express Saturday 30th July 1898

'Seldom has the Parish Church of Wadhurst been so crowded with such a large and fashionable congregation assembled to witness the marriage of Mr A E Roberts, son of the Reverend A J Roberts of Tidebrook to Miss Olive Maude Luck, youngest daughter of the Late F G Luck of 'The Olives' Wadhurst on Wednesday afternoon July 27th.

Owing to the recent death of Mr I D Walker, uncle of the Bride, who was for many years the captain of the Middlesex County Cricket Club, the wedding activities were to a certain extent curtailed; but the people amongst whom the Misses Luck have lived all their lives showed the esteem and affection in which they hold them by decorating the line of route with bunting of various description. The town of Wadhurst also presented a similarly gay appearance, near to the entrance of the Churchyard was a fine arch of evergreens and flowers surmounted by the words 'God bless the Bride and Bridegroom'. From thence to the Church door was erected an awning decorated with flags and evergreens, the whole having a very pretty effect. The path was covered with carpet. On entering the Church the Bridal party was met by the Reverends G G MacLean, A J Roberts, W May, Arthur Wace, C C Allen and Choir. The Hymn 'Fight the good fight with all Thy might' was then sung as a processional. The opening part of the ceremony was taken by the Vicar, Reverend G G Maclean. The Reverend W May, Rector of Brenchley, then proceeded with the marriage service. After the Deus the Reverend A Wace, Vicar of Haddiscoe, continued with the prayers and Reverend A J Roberts concluded with the Exhortation and Benediction. Then came the Hymn 'O perfect love' while the Bridal party proceeded to the Vestry. The Organist Mr A Knight played a Grand Chorus in D major after Handel by Alex Guilmont. On leaving the Vestry Mendelson's Wedding March was rendered on the organ and merry peals were rung, and proceeding to their carriages the Bridal party was deluged with Rose leaves from a number of girls dressed in white sashes, from Stonegate Sunday School.

The bride was given away by her cousin Colonel Luck in the unavoidable absence of her uncle Mr V E Walker owing to the death of his brother. She was attired in a lovely dress of ivory white satin trimmed with bébé ribbon with a chiffon and court train, and a very handsome Belgium lace veil fastened with a diamond star and orange blossom. She also wore a gold heart shaped locket and chain the Bridegroom's gift and a pearl bracelet, the gift of her uncle, and carried a lovely bouquet of Lilies of the valley and white Roses which was also the gift of the Bridegroom. The Bridesmaids were the Misses Fanny, Edith, Norah, Beatrice and Susie Luck, sisters of the Bride, and the Misses Maud and Ethel Roberts, sisters of the Bridegroom. They looked charming in white Bengaline silk and carried bouquets of white carnations, the gift of the Bride and Gold safety brooches with heart pendants, the gift of the Bridegroom. Mr Alfred Roberts, brother, acted as Best man.

After the ceremony a reception was held at The Olives but the guests were mainly family and close friends of the Bride and Bridegroom for the reasons mentioned above. Later in the day they left for London en route for Castle Howard, Yorkshire which has kindly been lent by the Earl and Countess of Carlisle for the Honeymoon.'

The list of gifts was enormous and included a family bible given by Olive's sisters, a bible, prayer and hymn book from Reverend Arthur H Courthope, silver sugar basin and sifter, a medicine chest, travelling clock, coffee pot, photo frame, book of Shakespeare, writing case, Haydn's Book of Dates, thimbles, a Lady's Companion, a cushion and rug, various cheques, an egg stand and cosy given by the tradesmen of Wadhurst, a leather blotter given by the Teachers and Scholars of Stonegate Sunday School and a double reading lamp from the indoor and outdoor servants at The Olives.

Presumably the newlyweds sailed for Canada shortly afterwards.

Olive would have taken some home comforts with her, but she would not have been prepared for the life that awaited her. The settlement would have been pretty isolated compared with her former home, and with much less than a quarter of the population of her home town perhaps very quiet too. We must remember that most of the inhabitants of Red Deer at that time would have been from all over Europe as well as the Canadian natives so it would have been very different to a quiet Sussex village!

By October or November of 1898 Olive was carrying her first child. We know from later events that she had the baby 145 kilometres away in the town of Calgary. It would have been a long trek, even by train, so this journey must have been planned beforehand. Red Deer was extremely primitive in those days, even the larger houses would probably have been without running water. Most women who had emigrated with their families would have had to rough it, taking their chances with childbirth and the help of the local women.

Olive would have been one of the luckier ones as far as everyday life was concerned. Her husband had purchased a large amount of land and would have employed servants to help with the upkeep of it and the home he had built. They would have been able to afford a midwife and doctor to attend the birth but, because Olive travelled such a distance to have the baby, it must suggest that the prospective parents considered it the safer option to have the baby in a more established town.

The next we hear of Olive is a small article in the Sussex Express.

Saturday 5th August 1899
Sudden death of Mrs A E Roberts - née Miss Olive Luck

'A few days since a telegram from Calgary British North America announced the birth of a son to Mr and Mrs Roberts and that all was well, the good news giving great satisfaction to all at The Olives, the Vicarage of Tidebrook and to their many friends in the neighbourhood. On Wednesday evening however quite a gloom was cast over the Parish by the very sad news that the happy Bride of just a year ago had passed away quite suddenly. Sympathy with the sorrowing friends in their bereavement is widespread throughout the neighbourhood.'

Sussex Express Saturday August 12th 1899

'The Misses Luck wish to express their thanks to all those in Wadhurst and neighbourhood who have shown so much kind sympathy for them in their trouble.'

Olive had died on the 2nd of August. After giving birth to her son Harold Luck Roberts on the 28th July 1899 (the day after her first wedding anniversary) she had contracted septicæmia probably as a direct consequence of unhygienic conditions or complications of the birth. She had lived for a further 6 days before succumbing. She was buried in Union cemetery, Calgary.

Her headstone reads

"Olive Maude Roberts October 11th, 1876 - August 2nd, 1899.

The Eternal God is thy refuge."

An obituary appears in the local paper:-

'The many friends of Mrs A.E. Roberts of Red Deer will regret to learn of her premature death which took place on Wednesday morning at her temporary residence on Stephen Avenue, Calgary.'

At the end of 1899 Olive's sisters presented the church with a beautiful stained glass window that had been dedicated to their youngest sister. It replaced the Baptistry window and can still be seen behind the Font which is located at the entrance of the Church.

The Luck children had lost their mother, their father in 1896 and another sister, Caroline Sophia, in 1892, aged just 23 years.

Albert returned home. On the 1901 census he is living with his father in Speldhurst. I have yet to find out what became of his son, Harold, although it is possible that he did not survive much longer than his mother. He does not seem to be in the Canadian or British Census for 1901.

Also in Speldhurst on the first of April 1901 was a Miss Dorothy Ann Nesfield. A 27 year old from Marylebone who was living with her mother Frances and her sister Margaret, 29. Her father Arthur had died when Dorothy was just 2. Albert and Dorothy were married at the end of 1901 and moved to Tunbridge Wells.

The 1903 Kelly's Directory has:

Albert E Roberts, 20 Court Rd, Tunbridge Wells.

And the 1914:

Albert Ernest Roberts Hollin (sic) House, Court road, Tunbridge Wells.

It seems that after the death of his young wife he sold up and came home. It seems a sad end to an exciting but brief adventure.

A GOOD WIFE   (Victorian)

What she should and yet should not be like

A Wife domestic, good and pure
Like snail should keep within her door
But not like snail in silver track
Place all her wealth upon her back.

A wife should be like echo true
Speak always when she's spoken to
But not like echo still be heard
Contending for the final word.

Like a town clock should be
Keep time and regularity
But not like clock harangue so clear
That all the town her voice may hear.

copied by Mrs L M Pope from an unknown Victorian book of household
hints

Wadhurst Churches in Victorian Times

Liz Kittermaster

The Parish Church of St. Peter and St. Paul

The church was built in the 1100s and the Norman tower is the only part which remains of this period. The lofty arched roof was built in the 1500s, from local and famous Sussex oak now over 500 years old. The real history of the church is pre-1837, which is fully covered by the very informative church guidebook.

By the Victorian times it was a thriving church which had had many additions over the years. It will have looked very much as it does today with the iron slabs on the floor denoting the wealthy ironmasters who lived in Wadhurst. One commemorating Judith Legas, the wife of an Ironmaster John Legas who lived at the Old Vicarage in the High Street, dated 1747, is interesting as at that time there does not appear to have been a vicarage; this lack caused problems. The then vicar, Rev Bush, who for some reason was unpopular and had been living in one of the Legas houses and moved to Little Pell, was mysteriously evicted from his dwelling, and was determined that future vicars would not be beholden to others for their accommodation. He raised enough funds to enable the then patrons of the living, Wadham College, Oxford, to endow a vicarage. No suitable building was found so George Luck, who had bought the Legas house was persuaded to sell it to the college for £350 in 1785. The house became The Vicarage for 200 years, until 1985 when the new vicarage was built.

The Rev Robert Barlow Gardiner was vicar from 1818 to 1846 and his brother Frederick gave the lectern to the church in memory of his widow Frances Anne. His eldest child Frances Elizabeth married William Courthope, Somerset Herald, Historian of Wadhurst and related to the Courthopes of Whiligh.

The east window is in memory of the Rev John Foley, d.1886, vicar of Wadhurst for 40 years. There is a brass on the wall in memory of his widow, d. 1898. Six of their children died of diphtheria in the 1850s and are commemorated in five windows, three on the north side and two on the south; only the latter retaining any of the original stained glass.

Another memorial of this time is on the west wall to John Tompsett, d.1820 and to his wife Ann,.d.1820, of Scrag Oak. The Tompsett family bought Scrag Oak from Nicholas Barham in 1741 and it remained in his family for 100 years.

WADHURST,

Sussex, Feb 21ˢᵗ 1931

Mr. H. Chapman

Dr. to Charles Bassett,

CHURCH SPIRE SHINGLER.

WHEELWRIGHT, CARPENTER, PAINTER, &c.

VANES REPAIRED, CLOCK DIALS PAINTED & RE-GILDED.

LIGHTNING CONDUCTORS FIXED, &c.

>◆◆◆◆◆

ESTIMATES GIVEN FOR REPAIRS.

Feb	14	Preparing & Erecting Fence		
	4	8 feet Oak Posts 6 × 4	1	6 0
	1	8 feet " " 6 × 6		12 0
	6	Orris Rails		10 0
	3	1 × 6 Oak Gravel Boards		5 6
	190	feet ¾ × 6 Weather Board		15 10
	24	feet 1 × 9 for Door		4 0
	1	Pair Reversible Gate Hinges		3 6
	1	Gothic Latch		3 8
	1	Gate Creosote		1 9
	1	Water Board for Front Door		1 0
		Haulage		5 0
		Labour 28¾ hrs @ 1/4	1	17 4
			£ 6	8 5

Received by
same date

T. A. Bassett

With Thanks

The oak benches in the porch were placed here in memory of Annora Watson Smyth, whose family lived at Wadhurst Castle from 1844 for about 90 years. The inscription reads:

In Loving Memory of Annora Violet Watson Smyth of this parish

Born October 23rd 1901 Died April 29th 1912

These seats her own wish given by her Mother

From The Sussex Express Fri May 12th 1912.

FUNERAL LAST THURSDAY. Daughter of W D WATSON SMYTH of WADHURST CASTLE. In August 1910 the dear child met with an accident, that led to a complication, necessitating an amputation and several dangerous operations. Since her accident she had been an invalid and bore her sufferings with great patience. She passed peacefully away in her sleep on April 29th. She was held in deep affection, and when out in her invalid car always had a bright smile and a nod for all the many children of her acquaintance. A special children's burial service was held by the Rev M Z Tankin. The hymn was 'Peace Perfect Peace'. The grave was beautifully lined with evergreens, narcissi and arabis. There were lots and lots of wreaths, Uncle Henry and Aunt Molly, Uncle Francis and Aunt Aggie, Uncle Henry, Nurse Steven's, All at Uplands, Etc. , etc.

[Kenneth Ascott records in 'The Education of Wadhurst' that Annora fell "when playing in a boat at the seaside"].

The upkeep of the church has continued through the ages, and it is said that the spire has been struck by lightning six times: 1575, 1595, 1631, 1679, 1850, and 1873! Re-shingling of the spire has been needed on a regular basis. The billhead opposite, though not Victorian, leads back to Queen Victoria's time. Although hampered by a steel caliper and special boot for a crippled leg, Charles Bassett spent most of his working life up steeples, until his death in 1923 aged 67. The re-shingling business was carried on by Thomas Bassett who, before his death in 1963 aged 77, had worked on over 200 churches in the home counties. His original workshop stood from 1890 on the old Pritchards Garage site [now the Little Park estate], where he was a wheelwright and coachbuilder, specializing in the traditional Sussex Wagon.

THE METHODIST CHURCH

In 1792 - the year after John Wesley died - we have the first records of a Methodist Society in Wadhurst - a total of 13 members led by a Robert Smith who was a local farmer. He also was instrumental in buying the first building '... used as a Chapel by the Society of Methodists in Connexion with the late Rev John Wesley.' An entry in the official records of Dissenting Meeting Houses licensed in Sussex dated 5th October 1824 reads as follows: 'A Schoolroom situated in the town and Parish of Wadhurst, the property of Simon

Clement'. Andrew Cory registered it in the Easter session 1825 in the Sussex Circuit. This building was on the site of the present day Youth Centre, and is shown on the Courthope Map 1840, which also shows John Maryon's Beer shop just behind it!

The years 1825 - 1870 showed considerable growth in numbers and activities as the building became the social centre for its members. In 1839 The Sussex Agricultural Express reported that the Annual Wesleyan Tea for the Sunday school was attended by 90 children. The East Sussex News dated 28th May 1869 also records another hint of the growth of members: "The United Methodist Free Church Benefit Society celebrated its 19th anniversary on the 20th instant. The members met at the Chapel at 2 o'clock when they received their dividend, at 3 o'clock, service was held, Rev. James Brown of Tonbridge preaching an admirable sermon. At 5 o'clock tea was provided in the Chapel of which 157 partook. A very pleasant day was spent."

The Methodist Church - Lower High Street

During this time a new group called The Bible Christians were both politically radical and deeply evangelical. They gained quite a foothold in Wadhurst and their protests concerning the labourers' demands for fair rents led to riots. History does not relate whether the Methodists got involved but there is a strong likelihood that they gave their support; The Bible Christians - or reformers as they were known - were very critical of Methodism. Therefore they lost several members and meetings were often accompanied by scuffles. The Sussex Agricultural Express of Feb.7th 1852 reported:

"On Sunday last at the Wesleyan Chapel, a Mrs Shaw from America but 15 years resident in London, addressed a numerous audience in the morning and evening and a liberal collection was made at the doors, but we regret to add that a most disgraceful scene occurred at the door so much so that a policeman was required to keep order!"

However by 1874 the Methodists had overcome any opposition and were able to begin the building which is still in use today. This new building with accommodation for 100 was estimated to cost £500 but the actual cost on completion was £801. A few additions have been made since but the general appearance of the building is the same as in the 1880s.

Methodist Chapels and churches are all linked to 'circuits'. Wadhurst was part of the Sussex Circuit, then the Ticehurst Circuit before becoming the centre of the Wadhurst Circuit. In 1974 it became part of the Tunbridge Wells Circuit.

THE BAPTIST CHURCHES

Strict and Particular Baptist Chapel at Shovers Green

At the beginning of the 19th century the Strict and Particular Baptist Chapel at Shovers Green was built for an expanding congregation at Burwash. Displaying its well kept appearance, the old Baptist chapel at Shovers Green, between Wadhurst and Ticehurst, was erected in 1817. Notwithstanding he was one of the 'brethren', the builder, Henry Kemp, had endless problems getting paid the £310 he had laid out. The chapel minute book records him as 'manifesting his hostile spirit' and 'pouring contempt on the church'. A year later legal proceedings against the chapel secured his payment. Somewhat whimsically the minutes record: 'Brs Hooker and Worsley went to Maidstone and paid Mr Kemp's lawyer (Thus the Lord appeared for us and delivered us from the hands of our enemies.)'

The most notable pastor was James Jones who, at his death in 1888, had been there forty-five years. His memorial stone is clearly visible in the photograph, next to his wife's. The chapel remained active and well attended right up to the 1970s, the last pastor being a Mr Honeysett of Tenterden. Today it has been converted into a private dwelling and restored to its former external smartness.

Rehoboth Chapel Pell Green - note the similarity with the Shovers Green chapel

Another Strict Baptist chapel - the Rehoboth Chapel - was built at Pell Green in 1824 - an attractive weather-boarded building. Yet it was some time before this that a fervent Baptist preacher, William Crouch, who felt the impulse to preach 'like a fire was in his bones' had persuaded Thomas Kemp, a Pell Green carpenter, to let him use the kitchen of his house for meetings. The Ministry was so popular that it was recognised as a church in 1818 with Crouch as the Pastor.

Soon it outgrew Thomas Kemp's house and in 1824 the two men decided to build the chapel on land belonging to Kemp. This is the building we see today although galleries were added in 1828 and 1831 and further extensions in 1831 and 1841. The cottage alongside dates from 1824.

The Baptist Chapel in the High Street

A third Baptist Chapel built in the High Street in about 1866 once stood on the corner of the street across from Lloyds Bank. It was converted for commercial use in the 1930s but retains a round window at the back, clearly proclaiming it to have been a place of Worship. It now provides the premises for Crittles, the Wadhurst greengrocer.

Whilst researching the Workhouse, Marriage Records were perused under the name Ticehurst Union (not we found connected with the Workhouse) and recorded banns and marriages of the Non-Conformist churches. An inordinate number were shown and an extremely high proportion were of Wadhurst residents both at the Shovers Green Chapel and the Pell Green one.

SOURCES

B. Harwood: *Rehoboth Particular Baptist Chapel, Pell Green, Wadhurst*, The Sussex Genealogist, Vol 4.

J Kinnison and B. Harwood, *Shovers Green Chapel, Wadhurst: The Past and the Pastors and Memorial Inscriptions*, op.cit Vol 3. No 2.

Alan Savidge and Oliver Mason: *Wadhurst - Town of the High Weald*

Rowland C Swift: *Methodism in Sussex and its influence in the life of the community (1756-1900)* and *1792-1992 '200 - Not Out'*

Extract from a set of account books covering the building of the Rehoboth Chapel - but starting in May 1819, when the Baptist congregation used Mr Kemp's kitchen and workshop.

Entries here include
Making a cricket bat 6d
5 days self 17/6
6¾ days boy 9/-
26½ feet of oak at 3/9^d p^r foot
Carriage of 81½ feet of timber £2-2-0
A jug 12/0
4 Spittoons 5/0

Timber was clearly expensive in Victorian times - a day's work for 'self' at 2/6 would not buy a foot of oak!

EDUCATION IN WADHURST
ROSEMARY POPE

The brief here is education in Victorian Wadhurst. However, it seems appropriate to mention that some education was taking place in the town prior to 1837. How many children benefited or which premises were used we were unable to ascertain.

At ESRO a school account book is held for the years 1826-61 and from these records can be traced the change/development of education from a National Day and Sunday School in 1827 to 1837 when Mr. E Gower was paid for work at the school and H Bull was paid for care of the school - he had previously been paid a salary for teaching. Then in February 1839 insurance for the new school building is paid of £14 and thereafter £13.6s.0d. annually until 1854.

These dates agree with the facts already known that a school was opened in 1837 at Pell Hill and a school opened in 1854 in the Lower High Street when Pell Hill closed.

ESRO records on education in Wadhurst show that a grant of land for use of the school was made by George Campion Courthope of Whiligh to the Reverend Robert Gardiner, vicar of Wadhurst. Also mentioned is that a piece of land in Wadhurst, formerly part of Great Pell Farm, was used to build a "school house by subscription".

There was further mention of an exchange of land - this time between G C Courthope Esq of Whiligh and the Rev. John Foley vicar of Wadhurst in June 1853.

Another entry showed land of half an acre, part of Townlands Farm, occupied by William Reed to the north. To the east the land was occupied by Charles Cox, south was a public footpath by the churchyard and west was land occupied by David Davies and William Reed. We found this entry confusing as to whether the above were boundaries to the land given or whether it was the land previously used by the said mentioned people. The churchyard footpath also left us wondering as to its mention here.

George Courthope grants the above land to the Reverend Foley in return of the previously given land for the Pell Hill school.

All the above entries confirm that the land for both buildings was given by George Courthope and that both schools were under the Church influence.

The Account Book lists annual individual donations which vary from 10s.6d. to £2.2s.0d. From these in 1827 rent is paid for a school room for girls, salaries for two teachers, coal, books including Bibles and Prayer Books,

Step Stile [Donkey Steps] - the route taken by Wadhurst children on their way to school at Pell Hill

and general maintenance of the building e.g. white-washing. During the period until 1837 two teachers were employed, one male and one female.

This interesting little book records that in 1837 (the opening of Pell Hill school) Frederic Fennell and Elizabeth Fennell are employed for the care of the school; they stay for five years as teachers. The yearly donations are increasing to £40 to £50 but in 1848 expenditure exceeds donations by about £2.

Stationery, Bibles, copybooks, knitting needles, maps, bottles of ink, coal and hop-poles for fuel, along with a chain clock are bought. The chimneys are swept and Mrs Luck cleans the school, with brooms and brushes for the purpose all listed in the expenditure.

How many children attended and what were they taught?

Kenneth Ascott in his book *Education of Wadhurst* mentioned Inspection Day 1844 when 60 boys and 80 girls were present and reading, writing, arithmetic and the catechism were the subjects inspected.

In 1854 the school in the Lower High Street opened with Mr. Bocking as the head. Although this was still a church building the state was gradually becoming more involved in education. Grants were provided and consequently inspections were instituted to see how the money was being spent.

Another book at ESRO contains the Diocesan Reports of Wadhurst Schools 1872-1892. During the period covered, inspections were carried out every April, but only looked at knowledge and reading from the Bible, the Prayer Book, catechism and repetition. The children also sang to the Inspector. Three schools (departments) were inspected, girls, boys and infants. On one occasion the Inspector remarked that the younger boys were noisy but generally the subject marks were good or very fair. Robert Blight (Inspector) writes

Miss Hannah Watson

"The tone and discipline of the school good". Mr. Bocking was still the headmaster.

Continuing with the subject of inspection, Miss Watson, in charge of the girls, "in every respect her work has been very successful" reported the Inspector in 1886. Miss Page, in charge of the infants, receives much praise "the infants behaved well and acquitted themselves in such a manner as to do credit to Miss Page". Another entry in 1883 said "the results do great credit to Mr. Bocking and his assistant Mr. Larcombe".

Finally, something gleaned from the school account book. In 1856 under donations was the following entry:-

Girls pence   £4.11s.4d.
Girls pence   £2. 9s.3d.
Girls pence   £1. 12s.3d.

No mention of boys contributing to their education, only the girls!

This reminded me that my Grandmother born in 1854 and who attended school in Goudhurst, Kent, had to pay 1d. a week for education. This was not a private school and she was one of a family of thirteen children.

Another entry in the account book during 1856 was "received for work done by girls £1.18s.3d". The writer wonders exactly what work the girls undertook - perhaps the knitting needles had been put to good use.

During the period there were some small private schools in Wadhurst - Miss Ashman at Hope Cottage (1851 census) and at Hill House in 1868 the Reverend Wace kept a preparatory school of about 9 to 10 boys. From the Courthope map and the 1841 Census, we know that Widow White taught at Gordon House [now part of Barnetts Bookshop].

The following information is again extracted from the census returns of 1841 through to 1901 and covers the area between the two tollgates.

1841
1 schoolmaster - Will Bull aged 50
1 schoolmistress - Susanna White aged 40
Children are not listed as scholars - and marital status of the teachers is not shown.

1851
2 schoolmistresses - Louisa Roberts aged 25, Elizabeth Ashby aged 17
no masters
104 children marked as scholars
one 11year old marked as an errand boy; one 13 year old as an agricultural labourer; one 14 year old as a railway labourer and one 14 year old girl as a servant at home.

1861
1 schoolmaster of the National School - Charles Bocking aged 35 married
3 schoolmistresses - Louiza Davis aged 35 married, Eliza Bouldiston aged 35, Louiza Waite aged 21
2 pupil teachers - William Waite aged 19, Elizabeth Waite aged 16
106 children marked as scholars
One family has a son of 11 and another of 14 working as agricultural labourers; there are four other 14 year olds working - an errand boy, a shoemaker, another agricultural labourer and an apprentice.

Education Act 1870 - a watershed in education provision.

1871

1 schoolmaster of the National School - Charles Bocking aged 45 married
3 schoolmistresses - Elizabeth Waite aged 25, Hannah Watson aged 26, Charlotte Page aged 24
1 pupil teacher - Isabel Franklin aged 16
1 monitoress - Mary Ann Brissenden aged 14
67 children marked as scholars but many children are unmarked. A 12 year old is working as a baker in the family firm (Carpenter), one 14 year old as an agricultural labourer and 2 girls of 14 are working, one as a milliner in a family of milliners (Mott) and one as a domestic servant.
A German governess from Kiel is employed by the Vicar's family (Foley).

Boys of the National School ~ 1877
Back row: at left Mr F W Larcombe, centre Mr Charles Bocking, right Mr A Goodall

1881

1 schoolmaster of the National School - Charles Bocking aged 55 married
3 schoolmistresses - Jane Bocking aged 32, Hannah Watson aged 35, Charlotte Page aged 34
3 assistant teachers - Sarah Wallis aged 22, Mary Wallis aged 18, Mary Bocking aged 14

2 elementary teachers - Alexander Goodall aged 22, Frederick Larcombe age 24
1 pupil teacher - Edith Fox aged 18
1 school governess - Elizabeth Waite aged 26
1 daily governess - Harriet Durrant aged 26
2 private governesses - Anna Howard aged 22, Frances Burfoot aged 25
70 children marked as scholars. A 13 year old boy was employed at the Castle, and another 13 year old boy at the Vicarage. There is a 13 year old groom, a 13 year old bricklayer's labourer and a 12 year old girl as a general servant.

1891
Charles Bocking has retired and Frederick Larcombe is the Headmaster, aged 34 married
2 assistant school masters - Edwin Williams aged 25, Alexander Goodall aged 32
3 female school teachers - Mary Annie Casterton aged 19, Bessie Barrow aged 22, Flora Boorman aged 23
2 schoolmistresses - Hannah Watson aged 46, Charlotte Page aged 44
1 assistant school mistress - Edith Brattle aged 20
no private governesses
78 children marked as scholars
two 13 year old general servants (girls)

1901
2 schoolmasters - Frederick Larcombe aged 44 married, Albert Knight aged 24 [also organist]
3 schoolmistresses - Hannah Watson aged 55, Charlotte Page aged 54, Mary Ann Larcombe aged 38 married
1 assistant mistress - Edith Train aged 19
2 governesses - Ida Helen Trickett aged 48, Emma Howard aged 34

Scholars not listed - presumably all children are now expected to attend school. However, there is a 13 year old office boy listed (his father is a P.C.) two 13 year old dressmakers (female) and a 13 year old telegraph boy.

Frederick Larcombe's two daughters, Gladys and Marjorie, were still teaching in Wadhurst in the late 1940s. Marjorie was the head at Cousley Wood School when it closed in 1949 and Gladys taught at Wadhurst Primary until she retired. Both were unmarried.

SOURCES

ESRO PAR498 25 - Wadhurst Education records

Kenneth Ascott: *The Education of Wadhurst*

Brian Harwood: *The High Weald in Old Photographs*

THE REMOVAL OF WADHURST'S POOREST

RACHEL RING

"Near to this (Town House) is a large edifice, lately used as the Workhouse, but now tenanted by different families. Wadhurst forms one of the parishes within the Ticehurst Union, and its aged and worn out poor are no longer permitted to linger out the remnant of their days in scenes familiar to them from infancy, and near to the spot where, when their toils are ended, they may rest with the generations of their ancestors, but they are now hurried off to a strange neighbourhood - away from those whom, having toiled for during their lives, they might expect relief from in their old age, - imprisoned rather than protected, under the provisions of a law, which can hardly be said to save the country even from the guilt of the murder of those, who having served it in their days of strength and vigour, became a burden upon it in those of their helplessness and old age; heretofore Charity watched over the interest of the poor and helpless, but Charity has fled before the face of this hideous Law, and necessity, - stern necessity alone compels the country to afford its poor, even that base subsistence, which willingly would be altogether with-holden"

This paragraph from William Courthope's journals (vol 26) was poignant enough for the writer to research what happened to Wadhurst's "poor" after the 1834 Poor Law Amendment Act heralded the combining of communities into unions and the closure of the Wadhurst Poorhouse.

At the same time there was a need to see how this Act that William Courthope spoke so scathingly of came about.

Help for the poor and needy has origins going back 450 years or more and the Poor Law Act remained pretty much the same until its revision in 1834. In 1833 Grey's Government introduced Lord Althorp's Factory Act which had far reaching measures for limiting the hours children spent working on the factory floor.

1833 was notable too as the government made its first education grant. Small as it was it led to the start of the state education system.

The following year, 1834, saw the reform of the Elizabethan Poor Law which had long since broken down. From the early 1800s the country had witnessed a growing mobility of its population; in the aftermath of the wars with France, the Industrial Revolution and farmers lowering wages, large numbers had been reduced to accepting poor relief whilst at the same time the local poor rates had escalated alarmingly.

The agricultural unrest of 1830 and 1831 undoubtedly was a major problem needing the Government's attention. Wages of eight or nine shillings a week could not support life and a higher minimum wage had to be enforced. Under the old system labourers had come to expect poor relief as an addition

81

to their wages. The Government appointed a Commission to examine the whole of the Poor Law and it was the Commissioners' report in 1834 that became one of the most important 19th century documents of British history.

The main recommendation was that able-bodied people should not be given 'outdoor relief' (outside the workhouse); this was to be reserved for the elderly and infirm. The 'Workhouse test' was to be adhered to rigorously in that anyone receiving aid from the rates must be prepared to enter a workhouse. To this end the institutions were not to be seen as desirable places of rest; the conditions inside were to be less attractive than "the situation of the independent labourer of the lowest class".

The Commission also had proposed education for pauper children in a separate workhouse with relief for the aged and infirm either by outdoor relief or in yet another separate establishment.

At this point the recommendation was for the formation of groups of parishes to form Unions with each maintaining a workhouse. Each Union would have paid officials, supervised by unpaid Guardians elected from the propertied classes.

The acceptance, or otherwise, of this Act was almost a north - south divide. The south with runs of better harvests, plus the growth of the railways and hence other employment, fairly peacefully accepted it, whereas in the north the textile workers had regarded out-relief as a kind of unemployment benefit when out of work during depressions.

The union workhouses were certainly less attractive than the situation of the lowest labourer and the unions could not support separate establishments for the various types of pauper. So all ages, sane or insane, were housed together. The rules separating men from women and married couples, lest they should produce more children and be a further burden to the Parish, were inhuman. Once in the workhouse inmates rarely left for fear of starvation outside. It should be mentioned here that no-one was forced into the workhouse, it was a voluntary decision albeit that in most cases there was no other choice.

Due to public pressure some of the worst aspects were gradually abolished but the horror of the workhouse and the applying for relief was a paramount factor in the lives of the poorest during the nineteenth century.

So it was with this background that eight parishes combined to form the Ticehurst Union: Bodiam, Burwash, Etchingham, Frant, Lamberhurst, Salehurst, Ticehurst and Wadhurst. Each parish had a given number of Guardians, the overseers of the workings of the Union Workhouse. These Guardians decided who could or could not actually be admitted to the workhouse from the poor of the parishes mentioned above. Each Parish was responsible financially for its own poor and paid accordingly for each pauper. Boundaries were firmly watched as no parish was prepared to finance a person from 'over the border' so to speak.

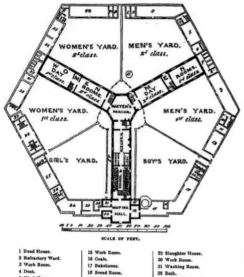

The first Annual Report of the Poor Law Commissioners in 1835 contained this hexagonal plan, sometimes referred to as the 'Kempthorne star'.

Sampson Kempthorne Workhouse design
For 300 paupers

1 Dead House.	15 Work Room.	29 Slaughter House.
2 Refractory Ward.	16 Coals.	30 Work Room.
3 Work Room.	17 Bakehouse.	31 Washing Room.
4 Dust.	18 Bread Room.	32 Bath.
5 Work Room.	19 Delivery Room.	33 Receiving Ward, 6 beds.
6 Washing Room.	20 Porter's Room.	34 Wash-house.
7 Receiving Ward, 6 beds.	21 Searching Room.	35 Laundry.
8 Bath.	22 Store.	36 Dust.
9 Work Room.	23 Potatoes.	37 Washing Room.
10 Dust.	24 Coals.	38 Work Room.:
11 Washing Room.	25 Receiving Ward, 4 beds.	39 Refractory Ward.
12 Flour and Mill Room.	26 Washing Room.	40 Dead House.
13 Washing Room.	27 Work Room.	41 Well.
14 Receiving Ward, 3 beds.	28 Piggery.	42 Passage.

Ticehurst Workhouse was designed by Sampson Kempthorne in a hexagonal style - a style used in the design of other such establishments. It was supposed to hold 300 inmates but from analysis of census records during Victoria's reign those numbers were never reached. The map [OS 1910 at ESRO - *see page 84*) shows the style of the building; exercise yards were shaded on the map within the spokes of the wheel.

The workhouse was built NE of Ticehurst on the Flimwell Road. Its address is now known as on Union Street and lies some few hundred yards after the Rosemary Lane turning. Nowadays Bewl Bridge Close is on the old site. Lying only one field away from the workhouse was the Hospital for Infectious Diseases although this was not built at exactly the same time. The Chapel in the front of the workhouse (known as the Iron Church) was an addition which we have not been able to date with any accuracy, although it is shown on several maps we studied. It was, however, dedicated by the Bishop of Chichester in August 1876. Other buildings are shown within the boundary and indeed these can been seen in aerial photographs of the 1950s when the site was known as Furze House.

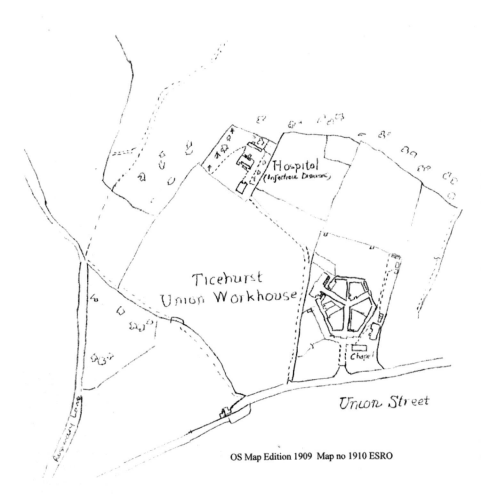

Ticehurst
Union Workhouse

Hospital
(Infectious Diseases)

Chapel

Union Street

OS Map Edition 1909 Map no 1910 ESRO

So Ticehurst union workhouse opened in 1839, and the first Guardians' Minutes written in March of that year but we have not been able to ascertain the number of inmates admitted at that date. Each parish within the Union had a certain number of elected Guardians - Wadhurst having three - and in the first volume of the Guardians' Minutes (Mar 1839- Dec 1840) the majority of the Guardians were farmers, two from Wadhurst, Mr John Tompsett of Scrag Oak and Mr. James Tompsett of Wenbans. Mr. William Delves, a farmer of Frant, was the presiding chairman. By the second meeting the representatives for Wadhurst were John Tompsett (previously mentioned) and Laurence Latter of Earls Farm, with George Courthope appointed chairman for the year. We have assumed that possibly the first meeting did not have full representation and Mr Delves was only acting chairman.

A sketch of Ticehurst union workhouse around 1880
On the right is the chapel (known as the Iron Church)

A fairly contemporary aerial view of the old workhouse. Note the design and compare to the designs on the previous pages. The site is now Bewl Bridge Close

Taken 20 years after Victoria's death but the workhouse appearance has changed little over 80 years

In this first Minute Book are listed the duties of Guardians:

1   Supervise all relief to poor
2   To appoint a clerk, treasurer, relieving officer and medical officer
3   Purchase supplies for workhouse and outdoor relief
4   To hear all applications for relief
5   To appoint an auditor

There were sometimes additional duties - such as the valuation of rateable property from 1862 to 1925. They also appointed school attendance committees. The births and deaths of inmates of the workhouse were also recorded and it is from this source that figures will be shown from the analysis of these books of Wadhurst's paupers.

It is interesting to note here that in the first week of the Guardians' Minutes that Wadhurst received out relief of cash £12.18s.6½d, and 101 gallons (!) of flour value £7.19s.11d. Of all the parishes Wadhurst has the highest relief, total £20.18s.5d, with Salehurst second at £19.15s..5d. It was noted that the total relief for Wadhurst falls over the period but it still receives the highest amount.

One other entry showed £30.11s.8¾d value of articles received in the workhouse and £31.16s.5d. value of articles consumed - a deficit already this early on.

In 1840 Wadhurst parish was charged 12s.3d. for the burial of Edward Blackman at Flimwell.

TICEHURST WORKHOUSE

From the Guardians' Book of Minutes dated 28th March 1839

The following Establishment Bills for the last quarter being examined and allowed, checks are drawn for the accounts set opposite the margin

Check total			Bill			Description
£	s	d	£	s	d	
			12	12	-	Waghorn Thos as per Contract for separating Men's Yards
			5	12	5	Do repairs and alterations at Workhouse
18	4	5				Check to Thos Waghorn for the above
			10	10	-	Piper Richard as per contract for chimney to board the school rooms
			2	4	11	Do repairs to ovens
12	14	11				Check to Rich'd Piper for the above
5	5	-				Keefes Executors - Stove & Ironmongery
6	12	-				Hedman George as per Contract for repairing iron pipes
			2	4	3	Harmer George - glazier
				4	5	Kemp Henry - putting new wires to flour mill
			1	15	9	Pullinger Thomas - hand cart and painting it
			3	13	11	Cooper Edward Blacksmith as per Bill
			1	1	-	Ditch John - preparing specifications & Estimate of Alterations
			1	6	3	Powell Thomas -
				9	9	Balcombe William - Cooper as per Bill
			1	13	10½	Noakes & Co - Furniture & Incidentals
			1	12	6	Barsley B Hay and Straw as per Bill
				2	1	Walker Joseph Do Horse hire
			1	1	-	Dengate Wm - Shaving & 2 Almanacks
				10	6½	Frazer Mary - for Mangling
			1	3	-	Childs Joseph - papering Master's Room & error in former bill
			1	18	6	Elliot Jeremiah - Incidentals
20	15	11				Check to Jeremiah Elliot to be applied as above
				5	6	Weekes John - Constable as per Bill
				9	6	Cheesman F - allowance as Witness & for use of Well
				14	-	Philcox & Baldock - Petty Sessions Fees as pros of Harvey
			8	6	6	Knight & Co - as per Bill for Stationary
				6	9	Ticehurst Wm (Battle) Do & Handbills
			7	17	2¾	Society for Promoting Christian Knowledge - Book
			2	15	9	Waters Geo Cranbrook - School Books etc
			2	0	1	Agricultural Express — Advertisements
						Maidstone Journal - Do (including last 2 quarters)
			1	14	11	William Hapley - Postages £1/5/5 Stationary 9/6
			2	2	4	T. B. Wiles Do & Do
			1	-	-	William Harris - Car & Parcels
				11	8	John Fuller - Paper supplied to Clerk of Union
				9	-	Mr E.W. Gilbert - auditor Postages - Stationary
			2	12	3½	Robert Tourney - Postages & Incidentals
40	11	5				Check to Rob Tourney to be applied as above
			9	5	-	A check to this amount is drawn in favour of William Brissenden for 20 Bushels of wheat supplied for flour mill, to be debited to establishment and credited to treasurers
			4	19	9	The value of 63 gallons of Flour at 1/7 per gallon ground at the flour mill and carried to provision account in 8th week of last quarter - ordered to be debited to invoice and credited to Establishment

A bill of costs of Mr Edward Collis & Co amounting to £7. 9s in an appeal between Wadhurst - Tonbridge as to the Settlement of a Pauper named Hilder is approved and allowed.

William Delves presiding chairman

When entering the workhouse inmates were stripped and bathed and then issued with a workhouse uniform. Their own clothes would be sanitised and kept with any other personal belongings in store until they left.

From the map of Ticehurst workhouse it is possible to see that there were various wings and these housed the different sexes and children. There were basic rooms for dining and the dormitories for sleeping; also in most work-houses there was a bakery, laundry, various areas for making clothes and shoe repair. Ticehurst certainly was surrounded by gardens and orchards where inmates would work. It had its own chapel, albeit some years after the main workhouse was built. It had to provide an area for education, a sick ward and a mortuary.

At this point, 1834, the classification of inmates shows that they were strictly segregated:

Aged or infirm men
Able bodied men, and youths above 13
Youths and boys above seven years old and under 13
Aged or infirm women
Able bodied women and girls above 16
Girls above seven years old and under 16
Children under 7 years of age

The daily routine for inmates as proposed by the Poor Law is best shown as follows:-

	Hour of rising	Interval for Breakfast	Time for setting to Work	Interval for Dinner	Time for leaving off Work	Interval for Supper	Time for going to Bed
25 Mar to 29 Sept	6 o'clock	From ½past 6 to 7	7 o'clock	From 12 to 1	6 o'clock	6 to 7	8
29 Sept to 25 Mar	7 o'clock	From ½past 7 to 8	8 o'clock	From 12 to 1	6 o'clock	6 to 7	8

Until 1842 meals were expected to be taken in silence. Prayers were said before breakfast and after supper and, in the case of Ticehurst, large numbers of the inmates went to Flimwell church each Sunday. It allowed them a few hours out of the workhouse albeit they were not free to go their own way.

Another clause appeared in the 1834 Act and that related to bastardy. All illegitimate children were to be the sole responsibility of their mothers until the age of 16. In the vast majority of cases these women were unable to sup-port themselves let alone any children and had no option but to enter the workhouse. The father thus became free of legal responsibility, or of disputed fatherhood; also the responsibility of not entering into improper relationships fell on the woman. This highly charged clause was rescinded 10 years later which meant that an unmarried mother could apply for an affiliation order against the father for her support and that of their child.

The inmates had a hard time and long hours of work (hence the name workhouse); many outside employers objected strongly to the cheap labour that the workhouse afforded and consequently lowered wages to their own employees thus worsening the financial status of the already poorest of the poor.

In the latter decades of the nineteenth century many women had been active within the Workhouse Visiting Society, some becoming Guardians, and they did a good deal to improve conditions within the Workhouse. By the end of the century the lowering to £5 of the property rental value enabled a Guardian to stand for election from the working classes.

The collection of poor rates, a form of local taxation, was made from the inhabitants of the parish and it was this that eventually evolved into the rating system. The poor-rate would in general be paid by the tenant of a property and not necessarily by the owner of it. There was much ill feeling by many of the lower working classes, who were often merely living just above subsistence level, at having to pay poor rates for people who in some cases were not prepared to work.

Unfortunately we have been unable to establish how many Wadhurst paupers entered the Ticehurst union workhouse when it opened in 1839 as nothing appears in the first Guardians' Minute Book of 28th March so we have had to scan the census records of the workhouse but even here the picture is incomplete as these records will only show the name of a person sleeping there on one given night; also we have access to only 4 decades to peruse.

In 1851   18 Wadhurst paupers were listed
   1871   27   do
   1891   13   do
   1901   7   do

An analysis of the occupations of the inmates in these census records is worth mentioning:

1851   4 Servants, 7 scholars (ages 4 to 14), 3 agricultural labourers
            1 sailor, 1 drover, 1 unknown and 1 bricklayer's labourer
1871   1 idiot, 5 labourers, 2 general servants, 11 scholars, 1 child age 1,
            1 carpenter, 1 lawyer, 1 veterinary surgeon, 1 carter,
            1 charwoman, 2 hop tyer and picker
1891   no occupations shown
1901   1 ret. navy [sic - *Royal Navy or navvy?*], 1 carpenter/journeyman,
            1 labourer, 4 scholars

Guardians of the Workhouse circa 1890

The birth places of a good many in the workhouse on the night of census taking covered people from such diverse places as Camberwell, Hitchen, Stratford-le-Bow, Bristol, Devon, Ireland, Trowbridge and Lancashire. Whether these inmates were 'men of the road' or passing through persons of little means we do not know. Each parish was responsible for its own paupers and quickly returned those who strayed over its borders to avoid any further expense. One person from Bristol, shown on the 1871 records, was a lawyer - not a profession one would have associated with the need of workhouse accommodation.

The next step was to inspect the Births and Deaths Register of the workhouse but again we could not start in 1839 as those records are not held at ESRO; they could have either been destroyed or are held at a place unknown to the people we have spoken to. The first records held start in 1852.

Whilst we hold names of all who were born or died in the workhouse, it is not important to list them here. In the 43 year period that records are maintained during Victoria's reign, 151 Wadhurst paupers died in the workhouse, but there would have been more during the preceding 13 years. No one year saw a significant rise in deaths, one to six being fairly consistent.

The Master, Mr Wilson, and the Matron, Miss E M L Smith - in the 1901 Census for the Workhouse

Turning to the births, 59 children were born in the workhouse during the same record keeping period. Out of these, 50 were illegitimate, and there was evidence of women returning to the workhouse for more than one illegitimate birthing or soon after the child's birth. All of the records analysed fell after the 1844 change in the 'Bastard Clause' so we must assume that the father had, or was supposed, to support the mother and child in some form despite her being in the workhouse.

The next source of information came from the Admissions and Discharge Register. Unfortunately, again full records were not held from the inception of the union workhouse, so we chose to look first at the year 1901, the year Queen Victoria died.

19 people were admitted during this year. The first entry was a large family of 8 but the father was discharged as infirm two days later; then a further entry only two months on showed he had died age 45 leaving a widow and 6 children. On the Discharge Register 6 left the workhouse, 3 were infirm, 1 died and 2 were requested discharges. It is probably important to mention again that no-one was forced to enter the workhouse, albeit the options of many poor people left no alternative.

This register was interestingly backed up by the Porters' Records covering 1897-1900. Everyone entering or leaving the workhouse for any reason was logged into this book. The destination of the inmate was shown along with the time outside. Patterns began to evolve of inmates regularly being admitted, discharged and readmitted. A certain amount of assumption has to be made as to the reason for this. Many reports of life in the workhouse show this was really the last resort of any pauper and once admitted a few days inside often led to a discharge request.

One character was in and out 8 times in one year and regularly left for a day "to Wadhurst" being gone for 8hrs 40 mins at a time. He was recorded as going to the doctor the day after one admission and was there for 4hrs 35 mins.

Was he a 'a man of the road'? He was certainly elderly and had been one of Wadhurst's paupers for many many years.

The Porters' Records and the Admissions and Discharge Book make heart-rending reading as to the poverty and ages of those entering the workhouse. Often a whole family of children was admitted and in many cases no records showed them leaving. Occasionally a parent left with perhaps the youngest child, the others being left inside.

Possibly one of the most distressing entries was a young family leaving and the next day being readmitted - what must this have been like for such young children? This also happened on several occasions to the children of other families.

The very epitome of the prim and proper Victorian gentlewoman: Miss Anne Hankey, formerly of Frant, at Holly Bank, Dale Hill, Ticehurst. The eldest daughter of George Hankey JP, Miss Hankey left Frant to be near her adopted work of caring for the under privileged at Ticehurst workhouse.

After Miss Hankey's death in February 1905 aged 61, the parish magazine recorded: "the Master and Matron and Chaplain of the Workhouse deeply lament the deprivation of an influence bright and loving, which made the inmates happier and better". Miss Hankey was buried with her family at Frant, but a monumental cross to her was erected in Ticehurst churchyard by subscription. A new harmonium was also purchased for the workhouse chapel.

On a lighter note: entries regularly occur showing large groups of inmates "going out". One entry on 4th June 1898 showed 16 children going to the circus at Ticehurst for 3hrs 15 mins. A month later 40 went to the Hawkhurst Flower Show for just over 5 hours; with flowers obviously being an attraction, whether to the Master or the inmates we shall never know; 42 went to the Ticehurst Show three weeks later. On the 5th November 16 went to Ticehurst bonfire and the year 1898 ended with 17 children going to Flimwell Church on Christmas Day. Other entries this year showed exeats of both males and females to Dale Hill.

Early in May 1899 seven female inmates went with the porter to Miss Hankey of Dale Hill. The following day Manleys Circus was at Ticehurst and 15 went to see it. This is approximately one year after the first entry, so we can assume that a circus was an annual event in Ticehurst to which inmates went. A busy time this week as two days later 25 went

Miss Hankey and her companion Miss Batey

with Cook to Miss Hankey at Dale Hill; 15 children and 10 female adults for 3hrs 20 mins.

One month later 21 men visited Miss Hankey for 3hrs 10 mins. This shows how the sexes rarely went out to the same event together.

A large outing to the Hawkhurst Flower Show follows on the 19th July when 30 adults, male and female, and 19 children were away for 5 hours 10 mins. The year goes on with another Flower Show at Ticehurst when 27 adults and 20 children attended, then 15 boys and girls with 8 adults went to Mrs Boyles at Oakham Farm. The last two events were 11 Boys to Dale Hill and then 9 adults and 12 children to the Ticehurst Bonfire on the 6th November.

So whilst times were undoubtedly hard for the poor people of the workhouse, occasionally social events took them away from their misery. It is interesting to read the Courier Newspaper entry of 21st July 1905 where Miss Hankey's benevolence is acknowledged and is obviously still going on after the period of our research.

In the four years covered by one of the Porters' Records (1897-1900) we have daily notes of the number of children leaving the workhouse to attend school in Flimwell departing at 8.30 and returning at 4.30. Between 11 and 19 children attended school and the log shows that they have approximately two weeks off at Christmas. It is interesting to note that the education of the

Dale Hill House, Hollybank around 1893

pauper children of the Ticehurst union does not take place in the workhouse as is the case in many of the documents read on the setting up of union workhouses.

The last comment to made from these records is that every Sunday 20 plus children go to Flimwell Church leaving at 10.20 week in, week out, and returning between 12.10 and 12.50. There seemed to be no mention of the number of any adults accompanying the children to church. As there was a chapel in the grounds of the workhouse maybe they attended services there.

Within the time limit set for this publication we cannot conclude this particular research without mentioning that as far as our research has led us to date, we find that the Wadhurst Poor House, prior to the 1834 Amendment Act, was on the Tithe Map of 1840 under plot 1831. The land owner was Thomas Barton and the property was described as a tenement and garden covering an area of 1 rood[1] and 29 perches.

---

[1] Like many units of land area, the acre was first thought of as a piece of land having certain dimensions. An acre was 40 perches long and 4 perches wide. (The king's perch was 5½ yards). A strip 40 perches long and 1 perch wide was a rood (not to be confused with the rod, a name from the Saxon gyrd used by the 13th century for the perch.) Not until much later did the acre began to be thought of in geometric terms, as so many square feet or square rods.

SOURCES

ESRO for all records about the Workhouse inmates and its functioning

Dennis Richards and J W Hunt: *An Illustrated History of Modern Britain 1783-1964* Longman 1967

G R Elton: *England under the Tudors* Methuen 1965

Census Records for the years 1841 to 1901

Internet - Workhouse Records and Archives

The Tithe Map of 1840 and the Tithe Award Book 1839 held at ESRO

Stan Cosham and Michael Harte: *Wadhurst - Then and Now*

Brian Harwood: *The High Weald in Old Photographs vols 1 and 2*

Alan Savidge and Oliver Mason: *Wadhurst Town of the High Weald*

OS maps ESRO

Trevor May: *The Victorian Workhouse* Shire Publications 2000

"The market is now held on each Tuesday, alternately (for 12 months together) at the two principal Inns, the Greyhound and the Queen's Head, and the Fair, during two days in the year, viz on the 29th April and on All Saints Day, the 1st November; on the last day of which month, St. Andrew's Day: the inhabitants have an ancient custom of hunting squirrels in the adjacent woods".

So records William Courthope in his journal (vol 26)
held at the College of Arms

THE RAILWAY AGE

NEIL ROSE

Monday, 1st September 1851 changed Wadhurst. The South Eastern Railway's station opened and its impact on the local community would have been immediate and far-reaching. The line had arrived a little over 20 years after Stephenson's *Rocket* had heralded the Railway Age.

Early days in Kent & Sussex

The 1830s and 1840s witnessed an explosion in the railway network throughout Britain. Purely local lines expanded into great trunk routes linking towns and cities. Brighton and Dover were two obvious places ripe for railway connections to London. The fashionable seaside resort of Brighton was only 50 miles from London, whilst Dover was the main cross-Channel packet port to France. Separate railway companies were set up to serve these towns. The S.E.R. completed its trunk route from London Bridge to Dover in 1844. At Government insistence it shared its route with the London and Brighton Railway southwards to Redhill before striking eastwards in an almost straight line via Tonbridge, reached in 1842, to Ashford and thence to Folkestone and Dover. Trains connected London to Brighton in 1841. It did not help that north of Redhill, ownership of the route was complex with trains running on the tracks of several companies.

By 1844 the S.E.R. was anxious to reach towns off its main line, considering itself the railway company to serve the area southeast of London, particularly Kent. It had bypassed the county town, so a branch from Paddock Wood to Maidstone opened in 1844. From Ashford a branch was extending northeast to Canterbury and Thanet. Tunbridge Wells and Hastings were two further towns that it sought to serve.

Tunbridge Wells had opposed plans for a branch line when first mooted in 1836: perhaps then the idea of a railway was too radical for the town's conservative inhabitants. In 1844, with "Railway Mania" sweeping the country, opinions had changed; the town was now enthusiastic for its own line. The S.E.R. saw financial benefits in serving the flourishing spa resort: the wealthy residents had already subscribed some 10% of the company's capital. Most unusually the 4½-mile line from Tonbridge opened on 20 September 1845, a mere seven weeks after the Act authorising its construction had received Royal Assent.

Building of the branch line had started in June 1844, with the support of landowners happy for the work to go ahead without waiting for legal authority. The line opened to a temporary station to the north of the town at Jackwoods Spring (near the present Grosvenor Bridge); the route included a tunnel near Tonbridge and a 26-arch brick viaduct over the Powder Mill valley, known as

97

Colebrook or Southborough viaduct. The extension to the permanent station at the foot of Mount Pleasant was opened late in 1846, the half-mile of line being largely in tunnel. Tunbridge Wells remained a terminus for another five years.

Twenty miles south of Wadhurst the ancient seaside town of Hastings, with its rapidly expanding new neighbour of St. Leonards, promised to be another lucrative market for the S.E.R. but access posed problems. On the south coast, the Brighton Company was extending like an inverted "T". To the west first to Shoreham, then Worthing and Chichester. To the east it had come to Lewes and onwards towards Hastings, arriving to the western outskirts of St. Leonards at Bulverhythe in November 1846. It took away from the S.E.R. all the Hastings traffic it had previously carried via Staplehurst, thence by coach.

Meanwhile, in 1845 the gap between Ashford and Hastings was filled by Parliament's adoption of plans put forward by the Brighton Company. The S.E.R. had proposed a similar route, considering the territory to be traversed as theirs. Whilst seen by Government as a strategic necessity, the Ashford - Hastings line was unlikely to be profitable as Rye was the only intermediate place of significance. The authorising Act contained powers for the transfer of the line, its construction and subsequent working, to the S.E.R: this was promptly done, largely as an astute political manoeuvre to gain support for more rewarding schemes further afield.

The S.E.R. obtained a route to Hastings, albeit extremely circuitous via Redhill and Ashford. It was hardly likely to abstract much business from the Brighton's much shorter route. The S.E.R. was not too concerned for it already had plans for a direct route to Hastings, using the Tunbridge Wells line under construction. The company also had ambitious plans for a new main line to Ashford, with a connection to Tonbridge, in a bid to avoid the dog's leg via Redhill and the congested shared route into London. The Ashford direct plans came to nothing, and S.E.R. trains were to continue to run via Redhill until 1868 when its new main line from Lewisham to Tonbridge, via Sevenoaks, opened. 1866/68 also saw the opening of Charing Cross and Cannon Street stations.

Parliamentary affairs

The S.E.R's 1844 Parliamentary bill to authorise the direct line from Tonbridge to Hastings was rejected save for that part between Tonbridge and Tunbridge Wells as construction work was already well advanced. The S.E.R. was to have greater success in the next Parliamentary session.

Undoubtedly there was plenty of local gossip and rumour in Wadhurst about a railway line. The first hard evidence would have been the arrival of surveying teams intent on finding a suitable route. The first such survey probably took place in the summer of 1844, followed by another in 1845 for the second, successful, Parliamentary submission. The resultant plans and sections

98

were substantially the same through the parish although the 1845 plans are much clearer.

Both showed a tunnel under Best Beech Hill, piercing the ridge, the water-shed between the Medway and Rother, at its narrowest point. The planned route was sinuous and sharply graded, with extensive earthworks. Wadhurst's proposed station was at the highest point on the line, adjacent to the turnpike to Tunbridge Wells. The only roads materially altered were Buckhurst Lane and at Scrag Oak. There is no contemporary evidence in railway sources to suggest that a route to the east of Wadhurst was ever contemplated and abandoned to avoid the Courthopes at Whiligh.

The Book of Reference accompanying the plans shows that four local land-owners were principally affected. The executors of the late Colonel By held much of the land along the proposed route between the parish boundary with Frant and Faircrouch Lane; thence to Best Beech Hill several parcels of land were owned by a James Bellamy. Alfred Playsted owned Snape Wood and much of the land southwards to the Ticehurst parish boundary, as did John Tompsett of Scrag Oak.

Bills for new railways progressed through several stages of scrutiny. Procedural correctness was vetted by the Board of Trade and many schemes got no further. Select railway committees of both Houses of Parliament then examined surviving bills in detail, not least to decide the merits of rival schemes. There was much concern that railways might despoil the countryside. If approved by the Commons' committee, the Lords examined them all over again. Witnesses were called – those for the schemes, opponents, engineers and traffic estimators – and were cross-examined by counsel.

Peter Barlow, the S.E.R's Engineer, was the prime witness before both Houses' committees examining the merits of the 1845 Tunbridge Wells to Hastings bill. He provided technical evidence, detailing features of the line through Wadhurst. Wadhurst tunnel would be 1,465 yards in length, have six working shafts during construction, with 75 ft. deep cuttings at either end. At the Frant boundary a viaduct 200 yards long, with 16 arches and 80 ft. high, would carry the line over a small tributary of the Teise. The line would run in front of Scrag Oak by a five-arch viaduct, 50 ft in height. Both viaducts were designed with brick piers and timber superstructures. He was rash enough to comment that the geological characteristics of the terrain were favourable for railway construction, being mainly sandstone with occasional outcrops of blue marl. He questioned whether it would be necessary to brick the sidewalls of Wadhurst tunnel, but then admitted his trial borings only went down for 26 ft. Although the hilly terrain meant a succession of cuttings and embankments, he said the costs could be kept down, as spoil would not have to be carried far from one to the other for tipping. The ruling gradient would be 1 in 132.

99

Barlow stated that the line was laid out for both through and local traffic, denying that he had avoided Wadhurst and Ticehurst which, being on ridges, had to be left some distance away. He based his evidence upon the Parliamentary plans and sections which provided some latitude as the line could be constructed up to 100 yards either side of the indicated centre line on the plan, with 5 ft. deviation in height also permitted.

Other witnesses, including the Marquis of Camden, spoke of the benefits that would accrue to the community. The railway would carry hops to the markets in Southwark - upwards of 10,000 acres of hops were said to be grown within six or seven miles of the line. In the return direction, rags to provide hop manure could be carried; they were bulky and thus expensive to transport. Coal cost 23/- per ton at Newenden wharf with carriage to Wadhurst adding a further 9/-. Corn, timber, livestock, fish, general provisions, building and road mending materials were all instanced as commodities that could be transported by rail.

A traffic estimator provided details of the potential goods and passenger traffic. The average population density per square mile was 211 for Sussex as a whole and 297 for all England. The 1841 population density of Wadhurst was 157, the same as Sussex if Lewes, Brighton and Chichester were excluded. The view was that the intermediate countryside served by the line was sparsely populated and would not be too remunerative. Nevertheless, the S.E.R. anticipated a 4% return on capital after working expenses were deducted. Opponents, including the Brighton Company (by now the London, Brighton & South Coast Railway), which saw its Hastings advantage fast disappearing, doubted whether revenue would exceed the expenses. A number of landowners objected to the compulsory purchase of their land.

The line was intended to serve Tunbridge Wells and Hastings, even if the latter was to be served by three routes. The opposition was insufficient to stop the bill successfully negotiating both Parliamentary committees and on 18 June 1846 Royal Assent was given to an "Act to authorise the S.E.R. to make a railway from Tonbridge Wells to join the Rye and Ashford Extension of the Brighton, Lewes and Hastings Railway near Hastings". This Act (9 & 10 Vict. c.64) also empowered the S.E.R. to make a branch along the Brede valley from Whatlington, near Battle, to join the Ashford to Hastings line west of Winchelsea: this line never materialised.

Seven years were allowed for completion, with powers to create £640,000 new capital and raise £213,300 by other borrowings to finance the construction of 26¼ miles of railway from Tunbridge Wells. An important provision in the Act was that the S.E.R. had to open the Ashford to Hastings line before that from Tunbridge Wells to ensure that the former route was not abandoned.

Building the line

Matters rested until January 1847 when the S.E.R. invited tenders for the execution and completion of works between Tunbridge Wells station and the turnpike road leading from Stonegate to Witherenden: this was subsequently extended to Robertsbridge, a distance of 15 miles. Eight tenders were received, ranging between £202,000 and £274,000. The lowest, that of Messrs Warton & Warden, was accepted.

Subsequent events might have proved rather different if the S.E.R. had not accepted the lowest estimate from an apparently unknown partnership. However, by 1847 money was becoming tight and economies had to prevail. The next lowest tender, of Messrs W. Hoof & Son at £234,000, was too big a jump. The pity was that Hoof was a proven and able contractor, and a respected employer, who had already undertaken satisfactory contracts for the S.E.R., including the Tunbridge Wells branch.

Warton & Warden commenced work almost immediately on this northern part of the line where the works were heaviest. The next 4 miles south of Robertsbridge would not be let until late in 1848 while the remainder to St. Leonards was not contracted until 1850.

Countrywide, tight financial conditions made it difficult to raise capital especially for lines with a doubtful potential return. Earlier expected profits had often turned out to be illusory, so the boom mania years had given way to caution and, in some instances, bust. In a contractor's market profits could be obtained in plenty where construction was straightforward: where difficulties might be expected contractors bid up their prices to a level that the railway companies could not afford.

Thus the S.E.R. experienced difficulty in obtaining satisfactory tenders for its Ashford - Hastings line that included four tunnels totalling more than two miles in extent. It attempted several stratagems to reduce costs including abandonment of the tunnelled section and making the lines single track. The company was eventually compelled to build both main routes in their entirety, and as double lines.

With the start of building, Wadhurst experienced a new phenomenon, an influx of an army of railway labourers - the 'Navvies' - and their families. Contrary to popular belief they were not predominantly Irish: many came from the south east of England, often local men glad to find employment. Maybe up to 500 men were employed on railway construction in the parish when the works were at their most extensive.

At the time of the 1851 census, six months before opening when construction was virtually complete, only 59 men were shown as being employed on construction in Wadhurst: of these 55 were labourers, one a civil engineer and one a surveyor. 10 had been born in Wadhurst of whom the majority lived at home, their fathers being agricultural labourers. Several came from East Anglia and just one from Ireland. The majority came from Kent and Sussex. Six labourers lived at Top of 'Tunnell', off Mayfield Lane. Other labourers' addresses were Snape Wood and Stream – 11 men, Town and Market Street – 9 men, White Hart –1 man, Rock Robin Hill, Savages Pitt and Little Durgates – 9 men.

If not living at home, most were locally lodged, while a minority lived in crude shanty encampments near to the railway works. In Wadhurst that near Snape Wood gave rise to the locality known as the Shant. At Stonegate, at Witherenden, there was a community living in shacks variously known as Tun Wells Br Railway Mudd Hut, Rail Cottage, Rail Hut, Tye Back House and the inevitable Railway Beershop. In the Gadd family, living at Lucks Cottage in the centre of Wadhurst, three sons worked as railway labourers. John Elvin and his sons James and Zecharia, all born in Norfolk, were labourers, John lived in Dewhurst Road, Wadhurst, Zecharia lodged in Etchingham whilst James lived in the shanty buildings at Witherenden. Labourers' ages ranged between 12 and 65, with the majority in their twenties. Wages would have been about 20/- (£1) for a full six-day week, about three times that of an agricultural labourer.

The labourers were a close-knit and sometimes unruly community. They were supposed to be controlled by railway policemen who, it was reported, often exceeded their powers thus creating bad feeling amongst the local population. Beer shops proliferated, often in the ownership of the railway sub-contractors. In Wadhurst the men frequented the Tunnell Hotel (in Durgates), the Fox in the Wood, Hare & Hounds, and the Sportsmans Inn; no doubt there were others, often unnamed. Local landowner Alfred Playsted retailed beer at the Snape Wood beershop: it is believed this became the 'Locomotive, later The Miners Arms at the time of the unsuccessful iron mining enterprise of 1857/58 nearby.

One labourer, John Brown, suffered the consequences of too much drink in December 1847: unable to walk home he was left to sleep it off in the tap room of a beer shop - he rolled into the fire and caught alight, luckily surviving. Living conditions could be hard. In September 1849 three cases of cholera were reported in Wadhurst, two labourers dying but a third recovered after drinking a pint of brandy at one sitting!

The heavy Wealden clay made local roads impassable. In December 1847 the *Sussex Express* noted the dreadful state of Wadhurst's roads – a 'quicksand' between Durgates and Cousley Wood. Maybe the turnpikes were better – the road from Tunbridge Wells had been made a turnpike in 1767 with its tolls being used to meet maintenance costs. Like canals and stagecoaches, the railway would kill the turnpikes; by 1870 most trusts had been wound up with responsibility passing to the local authority.

By September 1847 Peter Barlow reported that the shafts were down in Wadhurst tunnel and much of the heading complete. He employed a resident engineer, Richardson, to superintend the works. Nine months later work was sufficiently far advanced for bricklaying to be started in the tunnel and Mr. H. Austin of Durgates put in the first brick. The ceremony provided an opportunity for a large party of local residents, armed with candles, to venture through the headings.

Eighteen months later in the spring of 1849 work was progressing well with cuttings in a forward state. To assist with the construction, a locomotive was brought to Wadhurst, called *Samson*, arriving drawn by 30 horses. No doubt it created much local interest.

In March 1850 Barlow reported that the three tunnels in Warton & Warden's contract had been finished, as had two-thirds of the (estimated 1,575,788 cubic yards) earthworks, with one-third of the permanent way laid (9,483 yards out of a total length of 26,752 yards). £145,300 of work had been certified, with a further £57,300 needed to complete the contract.

Pickaxes, shovels, wheelbarrows, skips and black powder were the tools that, with labourers' muscles and the aid of horses, built the cuttings, embankments and tunnels. It is not surprising, therefore, that accidents were frequent, and often fatal. In January 1848 Charles Johnson, employed at the top of a tunnel shaft at Wadhurst as a baulksman receiving loaded skips as they were drawn up, slipped and fell 180 ft. to his death. Three months later 18-year old James Summerford, alias Brotherwood, employed driving wagons to a tip near Rock Robin Hill, was accidentally knocked down by a horse on to the rails to be fatally run over by his wagon.

Also in April 1848 one man was killed and two injured in the tunnel when powder they were packing into a blast hole exploded prematurely. The fourth death of 1848 was reported in November when Samuel Russell, a tip driver, slipped and was run over by his loaded wagon: his job was to unhook the horse from the wagon as it approached the end of the embankment where it was tipped to empty its contents. His and other inquests were conducted at the Greyhound Inn.

On 13 February 1851 the Ashford - Hastings line was eventually opened. The S.E.R. had been obliged to postpone payments of dividends to shareholders since 1849, a penalty stipulated in the line's Act in the event of more than three years elapsing to opening. A continuing dispute with the L.B.S.C.R. regarding access to Hastings would result in a blockade of the station soon after opening and much subsequent ill-will. Both companies employed separate staffs at Hastings for many years. Ultimately the two companies would reach understandings of sorts as to territory, which they often sought to breach, and agreed a division of receipts from stations jointly served, such as Hastings.

The S.E.R. was now able legally to finish the line from Tunbridge Wells, not before time as communities along the route were beginning to wonder if the railway would ever open. In March 1851 the Rev. John Foley, vicar of Wadhurst, sent petitions from local residents to the S.E.R. directors seeking a speedy conclusion of the works. Similar petitions were sent from the inhabitants of Frant, Ticehurst and Burwash.

The S.E.R. employed William Tress, an architect of Finsbury Square, London, to design suitable station buildings. He had already designed those along the Ashford - Hastings line. Tress's individual designs for solid stone or brick buildings were a credit to the S.E.R., which on other lines favoured much more basic timber structures. Today, his stations remain, with the exception of Hastings, little altered from his original plans and represent one of the finest series of small railway stations in the country; Battle is regarded as his gem.

In early April 1851 the S.E.R. contracted Mr. Edward Carter to build the five station buildings at Frant, Wadhurst, Witherenden [1], Etchingham and Robertsbridge at a cost of £5,071, as well as five lodges for level crossing keepers at £1,369. The original plans for Wadhurst were drawn in 1848 and show a building of red and white brick, with Caen stone dressing, symmetrical about a centre gable. The extension to include a larger booking office was built in the 1880s in the same style as the original.

Station in 1880s, showing building before extension added, early signalbox and signal and no footbridge.   *Neil Rose collection (ex Lens of Sutton)*

[1]   Ticehurst Road is the name by which Stonegate station was known from December 1851 until 16 June 1947 when it was renamed. For its first three months it was called Witherenden but this was altered when it was pointed out by the Ticehurst Guardians that there was no parish or village of that name.

Station construction was swift and although not completed until the end of the following January, progress was sufficiently far advanced in August 1851 for Captain Laffan of the Railway Department of the Board of Trade to inspect the line. His report is quoted in full:

Office of Commissioners of Railways   *29th August 1851*

Sir,

I have the honor to report to you, for the information of the Commissioners, that on the 27th instant, I inspected a portion of the Tonbridge and Hastings line of the S.E.R. Company extending from the Tunbridge Wells station to Robertsbridge - a distance of 14 miles and 68 chains.

The cuttings and embankments on this line are very heavy - one embankment being 76 feet in height, the other works consist of three tunnels, lined with brickwork, and apparently well finished, and of some bridges of small span crossing small streams or roads, there is little of any engineering interest.

The permanent way is laid partly with the ordinary cross sleepers, and partly with Mr. Barlow's patent iron chairs, the whole is in good order, and the iron way particularly runs very smooth.

I believe this line to be in a fit state to receive public traffic and I beg to recommend that permission be given to the Company to open it.

I have the honor to be, Sir, Your most obedient Servant,

(signed) R.M. Laffan   Captain, R.E.

Captain Laffan's report to Captain Simmons at the Board of Trade is surprisingly sketchy and, as events transpired, woefully inaccurate. It was sufficient for the S.E.R. to be allowed to open the line which it did, to Robertsbridge, three days later. No ceremony appears to have marked the occasion although a special train was run to London for the Great Exhibition in the Crystal Palace at Hyde Park.

The line subsequently opened to Battle on 1 January 1852 and throughout to St. Leonards (Bopeep Junction) on 1 February 1852 and thence into Hastings.

When it was fully opened a reporter from *The Times* presciently noted: "the line passes through a beautiful country in which great quantities of hops are grown. The district is diversified by hills and vales, and it is expected that when proper facilities are afforded it will become a favourite place of residence for persons having business in the metropolis".

In 1853 S.E.R. shareholders were told that the Tunbridge Wells branch had cost £293,071 and the Tunbridge Wells to Hastings branch £724,507, a total cost for the 31 miles between Tonbridge and Bopeep Junction of just over £1 million (about £3,300 a mile). Nearly £653,000 was spent on construction; £186,000 paid for the land (many owners struck a hard deal, with compensation often going to arbitration); permanent way accounted for another

£115,000. The stations – platforms, buildings, goods sheds – and crossings, from Tunbridge Wells to Battle, came to just £24,000.

The five miles of railway through Wadhurst differed in some respects from that planned. No viaduct was built on the Frant boundary as there was sufficient spoil available to build a huge embankment that became known as the 'Big Tip'. Wadhurst tunnel was 260 yards shorter than envisaged, and the line ran in a deep cutting behind Scrag Oak rather than in front, thus obviating the need for the planned viaduct at the Shant. Gradients, too, were much sharper than planned at 1-in-100 in many places. Wadhurst station stood at the top of a continuous bank nine miles long, descending to the floor of the Rother valley at Etchingham. Climbing this bank became a sore trial for up trains, particularly goods traffic, with the line between Snape Wood and the south end of Wadhurst tunnel nicknamed Poverty Corner, as engines often stopped there for want of steam.

Wadhurst tunnel as shown in The Illustrated London News, 14th February 1852   © Guildhall Library, City of London

Early days and problems arise

The first timetable of September 1851 shows three trains each way on weekdays, leaving Wadhurst for Tonbridge at 8.33 am, 1.08 pm and 6.53 pm, and arriving from Tonbridge at 9.59 am, 3.59 pm and 7.59 pm. On Sundays two trains ran each way morning and evening. The journey took 35 minutes from Tonbridge but varied between 33 and 47 minutes in the other direction.

Feeble brakes meant a cautious approach on the steep gradients descending into Tonbridge, where the branch ended in a siding facing east parallel to the main line. A complicated reversal was needed to gain the main line and the station, situated some way east of its current location. Tonbridge station was repositioned and a spur onto the Hastings branch, used ever since, was opened in mid-1857 thereby allowing through running of trains. In 1851 the shortest time to London, via Redhill, from Tonbridge was 1 hr 6 mins, although it could take 1 hr 50 mins for the 41 miles. Therefore the overall journey from Wadhurst to London Bridge took about 2½ hours.

The cost of travel between Wadhurst and London in 1852 ranged from 12/11 1st class return to 4/3 for a Parliamentary single, at a time when a typical agricultural wage was 6/8 a week.

The railway was a novelty for Wadhurst inhabitants; and hazardous to some. In July 1852 a young Wadhurst labourer was thrown out of the 3rd class open carriage he was travelling in from Tunbridge Wells, falling part way down the 'Big Tip' embankment. Apparently he had been foolhardy enough to sit on the edge of the carriage and lost his balance. He was fortunate to receive only cuts and bruises. Three months earlier Snape Wood was partly burnt, Alfred Playsted later receiving £6/10/- as compensation, including £1 for the men who extinguished the blaze.

Whilst the railway brought immediate benefits - coal was selling for 22/- a ton within a month of opening, 10/- less than before - all was not well with the line. Earthworks were incomplete, the track was faulty and ballasting insufficient. Derailments were frequent. George Courthope of Whiligh was in a train in October 1851 when it came off the rails at Snape Wood. Fortunately no one was injured and after an hour's delay the train continued on to Robertsbridge. If that wasn't enough, a second train also derailed near the same place later that day.

As was usual practice, Warton & Warden were responsible for maintaining their contract for one year after opening. As mentioned in Captain Laffan's report, part of the line was laid with "Mr. Barlow's patent iron chairs" which, instead of conventional transverse wooden sleepers or baulk timbers, supported short lengths of cast-iron rails on cast-iron chairs laid directly onto the ballast with tie-bars to keep the gauge. These were Peter Barlow's innovation and the S.E.R. adopted them for portions of new line. They were not a success, and Barlow resigned as Engineer in July 1851. They were rapidly removed from the main line but lingered on secondary lines for two more decades.

Thomas Drane, Barlow's successor, was sufficiently concerned about the state of the line between Tunbridge Wells and Robertsbridge that he ordered an overall reduction in train speed in February 1852. The S.E.R. Directors considered that much of Warton & Warden's work was defective and withheld their completion certificate, settlement not being reached until 1855.

In October 1852 George Wythes, contractor southwards from Roberts-bridge, was engaged to repair and maintain Warton & Warden's section. Over the next eighteen months he put down an additional six inches depth of ballast as "the quantity originally laid down was one fourth less than what is usually provided and it proved insufficient". Proper drainage was also provided with many additional culverts. Some of the sharper curves were considerably eased in the 1870s when the Barlow rails were finally replaced.

Following a fall of brickwork in Mountfield tunnel in March 1855, the Engineer inspected other tunnels on the line. Defects were found in Grove and Strawberry Hill tunnels, immediately south of Tunbridge Wells, so serious that the S.E.R. took out an action against Warton (where was Warden?) late in 1855 to recover damages for the "improper and insufficient construction" of the two tunnels.

When the case was eventually heard at the Guildhall, London in February 1861, it was stated that the Engineer had tested the tunnels by breaking holes through the walls and crowns to find the thickness of the brickwork. He found that generally there was only one ring of cemented brickwork instead of four as specified, bricks behind the cemented rings being laid 'in dry', i.e. without cement. Moreover, there were many spaces behind the brickwork which should have been filled. It was considered extremely fortunate that the tunnels had not collapsed.

The two tunnels had to be relined with a further two rings of brick and cement, thereby making them 18 inches narrower than planned. Fortunately for him, Richardson (the S.E.R's resident engineer during construction) was in Portugal and unable to give evidence. The jury found that there had been malpractice on the part of Warton's sub-contractors (and connivance?) and awarded the S.E.R. £8,500. Four months later the contractors insisted the tunnels be opened up for their inspection: the S.E.R. offered to accept £4,000, plus costs, or else would demand a new trial.

By April 1862, a year later, the Engineer reported that Wadhurst tunnel was found to be in a very bad state "in consequence of its original defective construction by the contractor, there being in many places only one ring of cemented brickwork instead of four". It is somewhat surprising that the condition was not discovered seven years earlier when Grove and Strawberry Hill tunnels were inspected. It is possible that the Engineer was re-examining all the tunnels in the presence of the contractors. In October 1862 work commenced on the repair and relining of the tunnel with extra rings of bricks, it being fully reopened the following May. Thus all three of Warton & Warden's tunnels had to be relined and so reduced in width which, in later years as the size of rolling stock generally increased, would impose stringent loading gauge restrictions on the Tonbridge to Hastings line.

Domestic affairs

Turning to local matters, in 1852 Wadhurst station had a staff of four men:

M.J. Macgregor	Station Master
Geo. F. Smith	Inspector of Gates
Charles Chester	Porter
John Humphrey	Porter

The nearest crossing gate was at Crowhurst Bridge, between Ticehurst Road and Etchingham, and the rest further south, so it is curious that the Inspector of Gates was based at Wadhurst. By 1860 the staff comprised:

Thomas Franks	Station Master
John Pitman	Porter
Levi Ovenden	Porter

Porter Ovenden left through illness on 12th November and was replaced the next day by John Pope. He only lasted 10 months before transferring to Etchingham, his successor being Ebenezer Oliver, who was clearly attracted by the pay of 12/- a week. Porter Akehurst was employed in 1863. By 1870 all these men had gone, being replaced by:

Edmund Morgan	Station Master
E Sunter	Signalman (replaced by E Buss during year)
W Wakeman	Signalman
E Taylor	Porter
J Little	Porter

Two years later, Messrs Morgan and Little had been replaced, with N. Newman added to the strength as Office Lad. Signalmen now replaced switchmen and police constables who had previously regulated the passage of trains.

The names between 1860-72 are taken from The S.E.R's *Register of Staff, Clothing and Furniture at Wadhurst Station* which is in the National Archives. The volume was found in the goods shed in 1954 and is the only one of its kind from the S.E.R. As well as listing the staff, the clothing issued to them and a schedule of all furniture and fittings, it also became two stationmasters' copybook of missives to Higher Authority. These records provide an insight into life at a country station, recorded by men unaccustomed to writing formally. Incidentally, stationmasters lived a peripatetic existence, moving around every couple of years seeking promotion to larger stations. Three of the entries in the register are noteworthy.

On 2nd May 1861 Station Master Franks reported that an officer of the Sussex Constabulary (No.72) and a Mr Box, a sheriff's officer from Tunbridge Wells, had arrived without warning and taken away Switchman Manklow from his post at the further end of Wadhurst tunnel into custody for debt. Manklow returned a few hours later.

On 2nd June 1863 his successor, James Hyde, wrote to no less a person than the General Manager at London Bridge. His letter is reproduced verbatim:-

"Sir having lost manny things off the platform at this station for some time past and finding myself daily something – sometimes money sometimes flowers, garden tools &c, I felt determined to watch for the guilty party and at ½ past four this morning the goods arrived and Guard Gammon had some empty trucks and one full one containing rubbish which was uncoupled nearly opposite my my bed room window – my window was open and I was looking out of it and in about 2 minutes Guard Gammon returned and went to the corner of the lamp room were four iron pans were covered over with a sheet. He removed three and took one carried to and put it into the truck containing the rubbish and while covering it over he looked up and saw me. I then said to him what he had put there he replied nothing. I said yes you have place some iron in the truck he then fetched a fold of sacks and covered it over. I then called Porter Akehurst to examine the truck which was instantly shunted back and then arranged up again for me to inspect but before I could get my clothes on the pan had been replaced the goods had gone and on me going to look for it I find the sheet thrown on one side and the pans in quite a different place than when I left the night before. I can also bring proof of the above and therefore leave the case for your decision and you will also find that Mr McGregor at Frant cannot even keep a birch broom on his station and Mr Wilson informed me that all his double flowers was cut off one morning supposed by the same men that runs the goods in fact nothing is safe on or near the platform. When goods arrives it matters not what it is, as regards Gammon the Guard I can explain more if required to. I am sir your Obedient Servant, James Hyde."

On 10th September the same year, Hyde duly reported

"One dog run over by 2.25 pm train opposite Goods Shed no other damage done except killing the said dog. The property belonging to Mr Joseph Smith at the Hotel".

It is a pity the entries stop in November 1863, for a month later an event arose that brought Wadhurst to the attention of the S.E.R's Directors. On Thursday 10th December a special train of 30 coaches hauled by two locomotives left London Bridge at 6.15 am, eventually stopping short of Wadhurst station. On alighting the passengers made their way along Three Oaks Lane to Turners Green where a suitable field was found for the prize-fight between Tom King and John Heenan. The police were called out and, seeking reinforcements, turned up at Etchingham (why there?) where they were unable to send a telegraph message immediately as the stationmaster made them wait their turn until other messages were first despatched. In January 1864 the Railway was reprimanded by the Board of Trade for running a special train carrying spectators to the prize-fight. The fight was illegal; running a train to a remote spot with spectators was not. Even so, the S.E.R. was summonsed to appear in court where they announced they would change their rules to give priority to urgent police messages.

Other lines

During the 1850s and 1860s several schemes were promoted for other lines in the parish serving Mayfield. More enterprising was the East Sussex Junction Railway of 1860 proposing a 12-mile line from Uckfield station (then terminus of a line from Lewes) via Buxted and Mark Cross to form a junction facing

Tunbridge Wells with the S.E.R. line at Watergates (bridge near Green Man farm). Another proposal ran from Watergates to Eastbourne. They all remained plans, fading into obscurity.

The Tonbridge to Hastings line acted as a boundary. South and west was L.B.S.C.R territory; Tunbridge Wells had been reached from East Grinstead in 1866 and was to become a significant 'frontier' L.B.S.C.R. terminus at the end of several routes. A single-track spur connected the L.B.S.C.R. and S.E.R. stations in Tunbridge Wells, although initially it was little used with passengers making their own way between the two stations. It was to become one of the busiest single lines in the country.

North and east of the line was S.E.R. territory, where the London, Chatham & Dover Railway challenged over a 40-year period. The fight for traffic nearly bankrupted both railways. On the impoverished S.E.R., trains were mostly uncomfortable, slow and almost always late, a situation hardly likely to endear itself to the travelling public. The rivalry only ended in 1899 when the railways agreed to pool resources and operate joint passenger, goods and steamship services. It was not a true amalgamation, both companies retaining their separate legal identities and directors, but the South Eastern & Chatham Railway that emerged was far better able to cope with changing traffic conditions during the early years of the twentieth century.

Serving the Community

Fortunately, the S.E.R's Hastings route, via Tunbridge Wells, was regarded as a main line. Wadhurst benefited as a result. In the summer of 1860 the best train service was the 3.24 pm from Wadhurst arriving in London at 5 pm. Wadhurst enjoyed a better service than both Frant and Ticehurst Road where only three of the four daily services stopped. By 1879 Wadhurst had six services from London on weekdays, the fastest being the afternoon express leaving Charing Cross at 4.05 pm, arriving at 5.21 pm, a journey time of 1 hr 16 mins via Cannon Street. The morning 'Parliamentary' leaving Charing Cross at 6 am managed to take 2 hrs 22 minutes, via Redhill: in the London direction Wadhurst was served by six trains, seven on Fridays. There were two Sunday services each way.

Wadhurst was similar to other S.E.R. intermediate stations with characteristic staggered platforms. Opposite each was a siding connecting directly to each other by small turntables at the platform ends; this allowed individual wagons to be moved from one siding to the other. These turntables disappeared at the turn of the century. The platforms were lower and rather shorter than they are today. Until 1898 passengers crossed the lines by a foot crossing. In that year a footbridge was erected (still surviving), built at a cost of £271, the steps leading to Faircrouch House being put in at the same time at the request of the owner, Mr. Symes. The up platform shelter was rebuilt in the early 1900s but plans to erect glazed awnings over the platforms came to naught on cost grounds.

Station at turn of the century with down express approaching. *Neil Rose collection*

The rather plain brick goods shed, built in 1852, adjoined the far end of the down platform. Of the three sidings in the goods yard, one passed through the shed running parallel to the platform almost up to the station building; a 4-ton crane was provided. Another siding served coal staithes in the lower part of the yard. During the course of a 24-hour period in the early 1900s some ten goods trains called at Wadhurst, used to sort wagons for other stations along the line. It received overflow wagons from the Forest Brick Works siding, between Frant and Tunbridge Wells that flourished for a dozen years or so.

In 1892 the S.E.R. invited tenders for modern signalling at Wadhurst. Messrs. Dutton & Co. of Worcester successfully tendered at £566, less a 2½% discount. A raised wooden cabin on the down platform contained a 22-lever frame. A ground frame, containing 8 levers, was installed to work the goods yard. The re-signalling was completed in April 1893 and the box remained in use until 1986.

In its first fifty years the railway's impact on Wadhurst, as elsewhere, would have been considerable. Time became important. No longer could time be approximate, clocks inaccurate, with regional variations. Clocks across the country now kept to a common time to aid railway timetabling. Not so important in Wadhurst, being close to the meridian, but significant elsewhere. The electric telegraph, forerunner of the telephone, brought news and messages from afield much more quickly than a runner or rider. Newspapers and mail could be despatched and received promptly. From an introverted, almost self-sufficient agricultural society, Wadhurst's horizons were broadened; residents had access to a countrywide railway network, available to all albeit at a price. There was much greater exposure to news, ideas and fashions. No longer was travel dictated by the speed of a horse: 60-70 mph by train was now commonplace, and in much greater comfort. The country had become much smaller. It was now possible to live in Wadhurst yet conduct a regular business elsewhere, especially in London. A population influx resulted, and associated with it the construction of villas and country houses for the wealthy about the parish.

Hops, timber and other locally produced commodities could be moved out easily to markets. In the other direction building materials, provisions and consumer goods could be imported, thereby allowing a greater degree of specialisation than hitherto. Haulage costs were lower. The goods yard now became a focal point in the community, the place where carters came for local distribution of goods and where coal and corn merchants established depots. Railways helped to achieve greater uniformity countrywide. Truckloads of stock bricks and slates gave rise to buildings and streets indistinguishable from one part of the country to another. George Street is a good example.

At Queen Victoria's death, railways were at their peak of importance. The internal combustion engine was in its infancy and road transport was not yet a threat. Maybe Wadhurst residents took their railway for granted in 1901 for, despite the S.E.R's failings, it had served them well for half a century. Journeys began and ended at the station; goods arrived and were despatched there. The railway station was the community's link with the wider world.

Sunday School outing c1906. View of station yard showing wagons in sidings and merchants' offices. *Bocking Collection, courtesy Wadhurst Parish Council*

THE RAILWAY AGE
PRIMARY & SECONDARY SOURCES

National Archive, Kew

South Eastern Railway Directors Minutes, Accounts and half-yearly Reports

SER Wadhurst Stn Register of staff, uniforms and furniture (RAIL 635/206)

Board of Trade, Railway Department:

> Inspectors' Reports
>
> Out letters 1845-1852

1851 Census

House of Lords Record Office

Evidence given to House of Commons and House of Lords Railway Committees in 1845 and 1846 on various bills

British Library Newspapers, Colindale

Herapeth's Railway & Commercial Journal 1843 - 1855

Guildhall Library, City of London

Local Acts [8 & 9 Vict c. 167 and 200; 9 & 10 Vict c.167]

The Illustrated London News

The Times

East Sussex Record Office, Lewes

Deposited plans and sections; associated Books of Reference

Sussex Express

Hastings Museum

Hastings & St. Leonards News

University of London Library

Course E. A: The evolution of the railway network of South England (2 vols) Ph.D Thesis 1958

East Sussex Census – 1851 Index Volumes 11, 12 & 13 compiled by C J Barnes

WADHURST - THE VICTORIAN YEARS

ROSEMARIE PEELING

On Tuesday 20th June 1837 at Kensington Palace, the 18-year old Princess Victoria was given the news that she was Queen of England, and from that day life for her and her subjects would never be the same.

In came the age of the Industrial Revolution and the rapid construction of the railways that would bring rural areas into close contact with London and the remoter cities in a way that had never been possible before.

Thus the railway came to Wadhurst and with it a prosperity that some locals had never known for, as well as working on the line and buildings, many inhabitants took railway labourers into their homes as lodgers, as a result of which babies were born and weddings were arranged hastily. Some local girls left with their sweethearts only to be abandoned a year or two later. Hotels flourished and local businesses also gained.

Wadhurst was at this time a bustling little Town. The main shopping area abounded with businesses of every sort; the inhabitants lived full lives and joined a variety of clubs and activities - you wonder how they ever had time to earn a living. Along with their own occupations they also held offices that served the community. People like Thomas Cooper who was a shoemaker but also held the post of Parish Clerk, Samuel Baldwin innkeeper who was also overseer[1] and Jacob Pitt also innkeeper and assistant overseer. And Henry Bull, who was living in the High Street in 1841, described himself as newspaper agent/vestry clerk and rate collector. He was still in the High Street in 1881 aged 81 years, describing himself as Registrar of Births and Deaths.

---

[1] Prior to the passing of the 1834 Poor Law Amendment Act, the administration and finance of poor relief and workhouses was, for the most part, organised at the parish level -- a situation which had been laid out by the 1601 statute "An Acte for the Reliefe of the Poore".

Local administration of the 1601 Act was conducted by the Vestry which was the governing body of a parish [the Vestry derived its name from the room where it usually met, which was originally where the priest put on his vestments]. The Vestry's membership comprised a Chairman [the Minister of the parish], the churchwardens, and a number of respected householders of the parish.

The officials who performed the assessment and collection of the poor-rates were called Overseers of which there were usually two or four in each parish. Overseers were appointed annually, subject to the approval of the local Justices.

In addition, churchwardens were able to act as ex-officio Overseers. Since the post was an honorary one Overseers received no remuneration for their work.

They kept records of funds, disbursements and distribution of clothing in rate books.

During this period in Wadhurst's history, some names run through the years like a thread. One such is Rev. John Foley who took over from Rev. Gardener in 1846; he arrived in Wadhurst at a time when the spiritual life was somewhat lifeless in the country parishes. But by his general influence he speedily infused a new vigour into it. Born in 1805 the son of Rev. John Foley, rector of Holt in Worcester, he was a man of great intellectual powers who worked tirelessly for the welfare of all. Such was the respect and affection felt for him that upon his death in October 1886 a memorial stained glass window was placed in the church to perpetuate his memory.

Another such name was Jabez Smith: for nearly 48 years he was postmaster of Wadhurst. He was born in Hailsham on 10th April 1818, the son of Henry and Ann Smith, and came to Wadhurst as a lad of 13 to be apprenticed to a currier. He was married on 14th May 1837 in Speldhurst to Elizabeth Barham of Brenchley both parties being not much more than 16 years old for in 1841 they are on the census as living at Primmers Green: Jabez currier aged 20 Elizabeth also 20 and son Jabez aged 2. By 1851 the family are at the Post Office and Jabez is described as a green grocer / postmaster. He was the only paid official and not only did all the office work himself, but also delivered all the letters. Jabez Jnr is not with them but their growing family now includes Alfred 10, Jason 7, Roland 5 and daughter Naomi 2. By 1861 Jabez is post master and butcher: their family is growing - Alfred, aged 20 assistant butcher, Rowland 15, Edward scholar aged 9 and sister Mary Annie 7. By 1871 Jabez and Elizabeth are in their fifties; Jabez has given up butchering and most of their children have left home but daughter Naomi is still there with her husband for she is one of the Wadhurst girls who married a rail worker. He is John Casterton, a plate layer from Rutland, and they have a 3-year old daughter Dora Jane. By 1891 Jabez is still postmaster living with Elizabeth and the Castertons in the Town, but his daughter's family have taken over many of the tasks; their youngest daughter is a teacher at Wadhurst School. He finally retired in 1900 after the death of his wife. He won the esteem and respect of all by his courteous and obliging manner. And on his retirement strong efforts were made to obtain for him a small pension but, owing to the rules of the service, these efforts proved ineffectual. Mr Smith was a constant attendant at the Shovers Green Baptist Chapel, and lived a temperate life. He was always in fairly good health until he caught a chill and passed away on Good Friday 1908. He died just short of his 89th birthday. His son Rowland who arranged the funeral held the post of overseer at this time.

It seems more than likely that Rowland and his siblings had belonged to the Band of Hope. There is a story in the Sussex Express Thursday 21st July 1881 of a treat for 120 children playing games for prizes on Band of Hope field, lent by Mr Rowland Smith, Mrs Brissenden and Mrs Pierson and helpers doing the tea, after which there was singing. The older children stayed for cricket, and

Mr. Spencer was praised for his organisation. There are many reports of these treats for children in the papers throughout the Victorian era. The whole Town seemed to get involved with cricket, and the players would range from the tradesmen of the high street to Mr. Watson Smyth of Wadhurst Castle who was a keen Wadhurst cricketer; for many years he gave the club the use of the ground free of charge.

What about the roads in Victorian times? Well a little story to illustrate that there were hold-ups and obstructions even before cars and lorries brought our roads to a standstill. Another Sussex Express story: in 1877 James Hall of Wadhurst was summoned for causing an obstruction on the free passage of the highway, at Wadhurst. "As Sergt. Avery was going through Corsley wood on his way to Lamberhurst he saw a clover-rubbing machine standing in the highway, about 4½ feet off the centre of the road. No horses were attached to the machine. There was a cloth thrown over it, which was flapping about loosely in the wind. The machine was so placed that it was an obstruction. The Sergeant saw a brewer's dray go by, and the driver of it had some trouble getting past. That was at half past eleven or so, when he passed on his way to Lamberhurst, and it was a little after three o'clock when he returned and saw it standing in the same place. He made inquiries and caused the machine to be drawn to Mr Ballards at Lamberhurst. James Hall admitted he drew the machine into the position on the road where it was found; he was fined - and paid .-. 10/- and 10/- costs."

Also from 1877 Sussex Express - we may ask ourselves if political correctness started at the Workhouse!

THE GUARDIANS AND THEIR CHAPLAIN

"The guardians of the Ticehurst Union have memorialised the local government board to remove the chaplain, the Rev H Harrison, Vicar of Kilndown, who has held the appointment for over twenty years. It appears that among the floral decorations in the iron chapel at Christmas was a small floral cross, about a foot in length, and which was suspended on the east wall of the building. And removed when the other decorations were taken away at the close of the festive season. The guardians objected to the use of this cross, and requested the chaplain to give them a written promise that he would not again send or use any cross in the iron chapel. This promise the Rev. gentleman refused to give, as degrading both to a priest of Christ's Church and to his personal character. This iron chapel or prayer room was opened by the bishop of Chichester last August. It had been erected by voluntary subscription, mainly through the exertions, continued for many years, of the Rev. Harrison; it appears that none of the Guardians attend the services in the chapel, and it is difficult to understand why they object to the use of the cross as a decoration in this chapel for the poor. When the custom of decorating churches at the principal festivals of the Church is now so common - in fact almost universal in this neighbourhood."

The census gives us an insight into the personal lives of the people of Wadhurst, in one house it gives the names of the inhabitants but gives as the occupation of one of the family "laid out in front room!" [And no, it's not the teenage son], and why does Harriet Wisdom at no time put her occupation on the census when she is on the payroll at Cousley Wood School as teacher? Or maybe Gideon gave the information and didn't think it important. When you look at the place of birth of husbands and wives, and birthplaces of their children, you realise that, even in the time before the railways were built, people travelled long distances. There are reports of suicides due to depression, windows being smashed in the Town by drunken middle-aged men and women, as in this Mark Cross court report August 16th 1851 in the Sussex Express - "Wadhurst wilful damage. William O'Grady broke windows at Wadhurst after drinking with workmen at the railway at Robertsbridge. His wife complained that she was beaten and ill-used by him; if she could get to London she could support both her and her child. O'Grady was sentenced to 14 days in Lewes Gaol, and his wife was given half a crown and her fare paid to London from the poor box."

~ In 1881 a Mr. Bennett was fined 6s and 4s 6d costs or 7 day's gaol for neglecting to send his child to school on 25th January.

From time to time the shops in the Town would close for an hour or two; shutters would be drawn and curtains closed in a mark of respect for the funeral of a much-respected citizen. And there were quite a few of them. Long processions of carriages would make their way to the church to be met at the gates by one of the clergy. And the graves were always lined with evergreens.

~ In March 1877 the Sporting Gazette announced under the heading

THE DEWHURST STUD

"That the entire breeding stock of Mr Thomas Gee will be sold off by auction by Messr's Tattersall, at Dewhurst Lodge, early in June, and his yearlings in Park Paddock, Newmarket, as usual, in the July meeting, so that another of the finest studs in England will be dispersed."

Thomas Gee was born about 1812 in Canterbury Kent. In October 1875 he inaugurated the Dewhurst Stakes and named it after his Dewhurst Stud in Wadhurst; it was his intention to establish a race that would attract horses of classic potential.

In this he was successful from the start; the first winner went on to win Britain's premier Classic the Derby in 1876. The first running of The Dewhurst Stakes was on 29th October 1875; the race, run over the last seven furlongs of the Rowley mile, had prize money of £300 put up by Mr Gee. The

Dewhurst Stakes is still run over 7 furlongs on the Rowley Mile at Newmarket.

As well as his horses Tom Gee was a well-known breeder of Jersey cows, most of which were imported direct from the island or purchased from other breeders such as Lord Braybrooke.

His first wife Judith - born in Bishops Burton, York - died in Wadhurst in 1873.

Widower Tom married, in Trinity Church, Nice, in the south of France on 25th March 1883 at the age of 71, Ellen Eliza 3rd daughter of William Henry Webley-Parry Esq. JP of Nyadd Trafane and Park-y-Gors Cardiganshire. The couple returned to Dewhurst Lodge where Thomas died on 24th April 1884. On his death his personal estate exceeded £187,000. To his wife he left £1,000, all his wines, liquors and consumable stores, three cows, three horses, two carriages and harness; he also leaves her, for life or for widowhood, Wadhurst Lodge, with the furniture, pictures, race cups, presentation and other plate and effects, and £1,500 per annum. After a few annuities he left the residue of his real estate to his children, and in default of children he settled the same on Arthur Bilby Pearson, the son of his executor.

In a notice in The Sussex Express September 1885 an advertisement appeared for an auction at Dewhurst Lodge on 24/25th September, by Messrs H J Austen and Son: luncheon being provided on the first day at 11am by ticket 1/6. The farm being let, the following were sold off: 43 head of pedigree Jersey Stock, of which 26 cows and heifers in calf, seven yearling heifers, 8 calves and two bulls. A flock of 185 pure bred Southdown sheep, comprising 92 ewes, 11 tegs and 85 lambs, four powerful upstanding cart horses, a very handsome grey mare with foal at foot, a useful grey cob, and a brown nag gelding, both quiet in harness and saddle, and a promising two-year old half bred filly; 37 head of swine. A splendid large retriever dog; a large quantity of saddlery and harness and colt-breaking tackle including bridles, headstalls, hobbles, muzzles, racing and riding saddles, sets of horse clothing, rugs and rollers, and stable fittings etc.

The agricultural implements and machinery comprise: 4½ inch wheel wagons, two Crosskill[2] wagons, spring van, four Crosskill carts, two manure carts, three liquid manure carts, pumps and hose, two water carts, iron ring and plane, hand rollers, sets of iron and wood barrows, corn and root drills, manure distributor, three mowing machines, two hay bedding machines, two horse rakes, timber nob with 6-feet wheels, Crosskill root washer, a number of galvanized iron water tanks and cisterns, sheep troughs, racks and hurdles, and a large and varied assortment of agricultural implements too numerous to mention.

[2] W. Crosskill & Sons of Eastgate, East Yorkshire were Cart & Wagon manufacturers; in the 1850s the manager was S. Copeland

Ellen Eliza Gee is still at Dewhurst House in 1891. With her is her niece Constance Wibley, and they seem to be living very comfortably indeed with a large number of servants including ladies maid and butler. One interesting point is that Ellen is aged 41 on this census, which means that when she married the 71-year-old Thomas Gee she was 33.

~ On Monday 7th January 1881 we read in the Kent and Sussex Courier that the Prince of Wales attended a private gathering at Wadhurst Park. He arrived by special coach at Wadhurst Station at 6.30 and immediately went to the Park to join a pheasant shoot. He stayed from Monday evening to Thursday noon, and during his stay was entertained by E Johnson's quadrille band.

~ May 6th 1898: it was reported that efforts were being made to restart the Tennis Club independently of the cricket club, for it was felt that not much if anything is being done for the Lady section of the community. The cricket club has offered, if a club can be formed by 1st July, to present all the tennis tackle in their possession. The difficulty of the ground has been overcome through the kindness of Mr. O T Corke.

In the same paper it states: that the principal shops in the Town have arranged to close at 3pm in the afternoon commencing from May the 11th and ending on September 7th.

Several interesting reports appeared in the Kent and Sussex Courier in January 1901 including:

~ "A public meeting is to be held on January 14th to discuss the proposal of the Crowborough water company to supply Wadhurst with Water. It is also proposed to pass resolutions as to the necessity of a pure Beer Bill. Mr Alex Court-Hope has consented to take the chair".

They clearly succeeded - an iron sign in Southview Road

~ In 1901 the dilapidated cottages at the entrance to the Churchyard were purchased by Dr. White on behalf of the Improvement Committee, the cottages realised £200 and were purchased with a view to pulling them down and the land used for the benefit of the parish, also to open up the view of the church and churchyard. It had also been suggested that it would be a great advantage to Wadhurst if a parish room, to be used for the purpose of lectures, technical classes, meetings etc., were erected on a portion of the site of these old cottages, as this would not distract from the view of the church and churchyard. The want of such a building had for some time been felt.

~ There was also a report of a 'pretty' wedding taking place at the Parish Church on New Year's Day, between Miss Kate Skinner [eldest] daughter of Mr W A Skinner of Durgates, and Mr H Ford of Ticehurst. The Rev. G. G. MacLean officiated. "The Bride was attired in a costume of brown cloth. Trimmed with white silk and sprays of orange blossom. She carried a shower bouquet. The Bride was given away by her brother. And was attended by her sisters, Miss Lucy and Miss Alice Skinner, who wore dresses of heliotrope cloth, trimmed with velvet and chiffon to match, and gold cord. Their hats were trimmed with black and cream chiffon. And they carried lovely bouquets The Bridegroom's best man was Mr. Walter Ford. The wedding breakfast was held at the house of the bride's father, at Durgates. The newly married couple left in the afternoon for Hitchin, where they intend to spend their honeymoon. The wedding presents were numerous and useful. Bride to Bridegroom gold links. Bridegroom to Bride, fur muff. Bridegroom to Bride-maids, heart shaped gold locket and chain."

Let us take our leave of Victorian Wadhurst on a happy note. Also from The Courier January 1901.

~ "The members of the Wadhurst Quadrille Class gave their first ball for the season on Wednesday evening at The Greyhound Hotel. The large Ballroom was very tastefully decorated, Mr Wm Ballard [*a local blacksmith*] proved an admirable M C and Miss A Newington pianist; there were between 50 and 60 there."

And so as the music fades and a new era begins many elderly residents have taken their leave and those that are left reminisce about the past. We welcome the Edwardian reign whatever that might bring.

Pilbeam's Forge in St James' Square

THE BLACKSMITHS AND WHEELWRIGHTS OF WADHURST

JOHN MILLETT

Before the advent of the motor car and the tractor on the rural scene in the early twentieth century, the horse reigned supreme, and where the horse was there was a plentiful backup of blacksmiths, farriers and wheelwrights. Our village sign reminds us of the importance of the anvil in Wadhurst, and our village forefathers would have awakened to the sound of the blacksmith at work, because he was always an early riser.

Today, sadly, the traditional forges have gone from Wadhurst, but we are reminded of the site of some of them by Forge House at Sparrows Green, Forge Cottage in St James' Square and another in Cousley Wood, Forge House at Best Beech, and Bassetts Forge in Durgates.

In the 1851 census index there are 15 blacksmiths listed as working in the Parish of Wadhurst, and also 3 listed as wheelwrights. The forge would usually have an adjacent wheelwrights, either under separate ownership, or as part of the forge. At the forge, farm implements and carts would be made and repaired, and new iron tyres would be forged and fitted to the wheels. The wheelwrights would make and fit the axles and wheels.

Not every blacksmith was a farrier, shoeing horses, but every forge would certainly have one or more. Most working horses wore shoes, and certainly all riding horses. These shoes would need replacing every 10 to 12 weeks, and this would mostly be done in the forge, but the farrier would also go out, particularly to upper class houses, to fit shoes. Bigger estates, eg. Bayham and Penshurst had their own forges, but Whiligh used the village blacksmith.

The site of six forges can be identified. As already mentioned, there was the forge at Best Beech, occupied until a few years ago by Eatons garage, the forge in St James' Square, next to the Methodist Church, the Sparrows Green forge where the site is now built on as Rosemary Lages solicitors, the forge at Cousley Wood opposite the Old Vine, and Bassetts Forge in Durgates. There is also the site of a forge shown on old maps on the track from the railway crossing in Snape Woods to Snape Lane. In the 1851 census a Frederick Till and his employee Frederick Stapely, blacksmiths, are listed as living at Little Snape, and Simeon Gibb, wheelwright living at Snape Wood may also have worked at the forge.

A William Funnell, blacksmith, is listed in 1851 as 'top of Railway Tunnel'; he probably worked as a railway blacksmith. There was a small group of railway people at 'Top of Tunnel' in March 1851, but by then the railway work was largely finished in the Wadhurst area.

Probably the oldest forge in Wadhurst was the one in Sparrows Green. Parts of Forge House date back to Tudor times, but the first recorded blacksmith owner occupier was John Elliot 1735 - 1773. The next recorded blacksmith was Matthew Ballard 1799 - 1827. The house was extended into the forge in the early1800s. From 1827 - 1910 the property was owned by the Whiligh Estate, and during the whole of that time the Hemsley family were working tenants. The family had previously had the forge in Isfield. In 1851 four of the family were listed as blacksmiths, and they also employed 2 men, so it was quite a flourishing business. There is an interesting note about the forge in "*The Story of Wadhurst*" edited by Alfred Wace in 1924 - "Sparrows Green, a pretty hamlet in the old days with its old cottages facing the Red Lion. The blacksmiths on one side of the road, and as often in the old days, the wheelwright on the other where old Barham worked under the walnut tree."

In 1910 the property was bought from the Whiligh Estate by Albert Hemsley, who is recorded as having worked as a blacksmith in Tunbridge Wells in 1891. Albert's father William had died in 1908, and Albert bought the freehold on a £600 mortgage and immediately built 3 more houses that are still adjacent to the site. By this time there was only local agricultural trade left, and in 1914 he sold up with £195 proceeds. The property was sold to William John Piper who was a plumber. Subsequently it is recorded that Albert and his family emigrated to America in 1919, his wife's mother living out there. His fortunes must have improved as they travelled first class on the SS Saxonia, and apparently possessed $2,600, probably enough to purchase a small property.

Another old forge in Wadhurst was the one in St James' Square [*p. 122*]. The Courthope map of Wadhurst in the 1840s shows Forge Cottage divided into two, with William Reed the blacksmith living next to the forge, and Richard Hamilton a tailor living in the other half. The property belonged to the Courthope Estate. It appears that Reed had a thriving business also; the 1851 census states that he employed 2 men, and there are also 2 nineteen year old apprentices who also worked in Town, probably for Reed. The Census also lists 2 other William Reeds, so life must have been a bit confusing! The blacksmiths' son, aged 13, was also William; the third William, at 46 two years older, was listed as farmer and victualler at the Greyhound.

Interestingly, the family history of George Cutbush, as related by Emma Richardson in Newsletter 6 of the Wadhurst History Society, shows that George's widow Elisabeth married widower William Reed in 1850, and in doing so broke a condition of her late husband's will that she remained "faithful to his memory and should not remarry"! In doing so she appears to have forgone a considerable income.

William snr died in1891 aged 74, by which time his son William was the blacksmith. The family had expanded with children from all three marriages and the cottage must have been quite crowded!

In 1899 Thomas Pilbeam took over the forge where he appeared to have been working for some time, his son Thomas jnr was born in the cottage (other half?) in 1893. A list of stock, tools, and fixtures, dated October 31st 1899 makes interesting reading, and shows that he paid £65 -13 -1 for everything listed!

Thomas snr. married Helen who was the daughter of David Page, also a blacksmith, shown in the 1851 census as working for George Gallop at the Best Beech Forge.

The picture dated around 1910 [p 106], shows the two Thomas Pilbeams standing outside the forge on the day that young Thomas finished his apprenticeship. The sign on the wall says 'Pilbeam and Son shoe and general smiths'.

Thomas Pilbeam jnr. had a large family, 5 sons and 2 daughters, but unfortunately 2 sons were killed together on that fateful day in May 1915 at the Battle of Aubers Ridge.

As general blacksmith's work declined, Thomas jnr diversified, he kept pigs behind the cottage and also started a coal business, buying his first lorry in 1935, he also used to hire out horse and carts to the council for road mending. However despite all this, he finally closed the forge in 1937 and sold the coal business to Lavenders in 1938. Thomas died in 1970.

The forge at Best Beech belonged to the Gallop family who were tenants of the Manor of Mayfield Baker. George Gallop and his wife Phoebe came from Waldron and the 1851 census shows that George the blacksmith employed another blacksmith David Page mentioned earlier. Also listed as working at Best Beech Hill are 2 wheelwrights, Henry Gibb who employed an Albert Turner, but whether this business was part of the forge is not known.

Interestingly, the census also lists a Henry Gallop blacksmith coming from Waldron, and the same age as George, employing one, at Butchers Cross, Rotherfield. This looks like twin brothers!

The Gallops were prolific. Unfortunately Phoebe died, but George remarried, and from 2 wives he produced 6 children. Edwin, his second son, became a blacksmith and entered into the tenancy agreement in 1902, even though George had died in 1895 aged 72.

Edwin was even more prolific than his father, producing 5 sons and 2 daughters. Three sons became blacksmiths, Albert and Frank entering into the tenancy agreement in 1925 following Edwin's death in 1924, and George the eldest son opened a forge in Cousley Wood.

Frank Gallop unfortunately died at the relatively young age of 61 in 1946 and Albert bought out his widow Annie's share of the tenancy in 1948. However by this time he was already 69 and, what with age and the fall off in work, the business became rather run down and soon closed.

In 1952 Bill and Tom Eaton bought the forge buildings; they established Eatons Garage, that too has succumbed to the march of time, and the site has been built over.

Frank's son George Gallop jnr was a blacksmith's apprentice aged 15 according to the census of 1891 and a document dated 1925 relating to the tenancy of the Best Beech Forge gives his address as Cousley Wood. He probably moved there around 1895 and either took over or started the forge there. The old forge building still stands in the garden of the very attractive Ketley Cottage, almost opposite the Old Vine. Ketley Cottage was moved to its present site from Ketley Lane when the Bewl Reservoir was built, and was re-erected between Elder Cottage, which was George Gallop's house, and the forge.

George was a farrier and blacksmith and the establishment was quite busy. There was no wheelwright's shop; perhaps he worked with the one at Best Beech. It is not known how many worked in the forge with George, but he was known as 'old Gallop' by the locals, and could be seen working at the anvil until the forge finally closed shortly after the war when George was in his 70s.

The forge that survived the longest in Wadhurst was Bassetts Forge in Durgates, which finally closed with the retirement of Rodney Bassett, the grandson of the founder, in 1988. In fact it still survives in name with the development on the site, and the preservation of the old coach house, renovated into domestic accommodation.

The business was started by James Bassett a wheelwright in 1881; his shop was believed to have been where the Shell garage is now in Durgates. As the business grew he moved into bigger accommodation in what is now the Durgates Industrial Estate and the wheelwrights developed into a coach builder and wheelwright. The original coachbuilder's shop can still be seen on the left as one goes down into the Industrial Estate. Ledgers and account books of the firm are held in the Record Office in Lewes and show a thriving concern.

The billhead read:

Dr. to J. Bassett
Coach Builder and Painter
Wheelwright etc
Durgates Wadhurst.

Every description of carriage repaired on the most reasonable terms.

Some of those terms are shown in entries in the customer account book:-

1899   pair dung cart wheels with ring tyres £2 - 10 - 0
new axle 12 - 6

1900 -   Dr. Fazan (the father of Dr. Fazan of Fazan Court)
Repair hooded gig - all new trimming to inside of hood. 2 cushions and driving box
Sewing head leather where wanted. Splicing hoop sticks. Trimming with best brown cloth.
5 lbs extra horse hair £ 8 -0 -0

James Bassett had 3 sons working with him in the firm: Charlie who was a wheelwright, William and John (always known as Jack) were the blacksmiths. James had a brother Charles who was a builder and spire shingler and Jack, apparently quite ambitious, went to work for him to earn some good money, returning to the firm in 1902. He had originally started working for his father from the age of 13, working from 4 am - 8 pm just for his keep!

Around 1902 Jack borrowed some money from his uncle, and together with the money he had earned bought a plot of wooded ground on the opposite side of the road from his father's establishment, from the owners of Wadhurst Castle. He cleared this site and built the forge, and started shoeing horses! In due course a new wheelwright's shop was built alongside, and finally a fine carriage house, and his father James and brothers Charlie and William moved the business across the road. A pair of cottages was built alongside the forge, Charlie living in the left side and Jack in the right side.

Jack had only one son, Rodney, born in 1908 who lived all his life in the cottage with his own family and his father, until Jack's death in the late 1960s. Jack in fact continued pottering in the forge into his 80s; when interviewed at 86 he claimed to still rise at 5 am and to work round the clock, but had to sit down sometimes!

The business was exceedingly busy; a picture in 1904 shows 10 people working in the firm, the new billhead now read:

Dr. to J. Bassett
Carriage, Cart, and Van builder
Spring and Tyre Smith
Wheelwright in all branches
Horses carefully shod

One reminiscence of old Jack in the interview already mentioned is that he remembered being sent across the road to the Brewery in Durgates to buy beer at 1 shilling a gallon to give to the carters while they waited for their horses to be shod.

Jack and Rodney were the farriers, assisted by others. It is believed that at one time one of the Gallop family of Best Beech worked there. They were very busy, even following the decline of the working horse; in 1967 they had 300 - 400 horses on their books, and on average made 140 shoes a week. Of course many of these horses were visited at home by Rodney or his apprentice.

In the days of the draught horse, coal would be brought up from the station by cart; sometimes the horse would cast a shoe and the farrier would be sent for.

The carriage house was also very busy, both in repairs and renovations, and also in making many new carriages and carts. There were books of designs to be consulted and anything could be made to order, taking 6 - 8 weeks to complete a fine carriage. The vehicle was built at ground level, and then raised on a lift to the first floor for painting. At first the upper floor was open to the elements, but it was later roofed over to preserve the ropes of the lift. A total of 4 or 5 people worked in the carriage house.

Finally a word about the art of the wheelwright. A wheel was made from 3 types of wood: the rim was of ash, the spokes of oak, and the hub of elm. If the spokes of a wheel became loose the wheel would be immersed in water for some time to swell the spokes. An iron tyre made by the blacksmith was then put on the wheel. The wheel was laid on the round tyring platform, and the almost red hot tyre was picked off the forge by two men with tongs and fitted to the wheel. The hot iron would of course expand so that it would fit over the wood rim and it was then immediately doused in water to shrink it onto the wheel and prevent the wood burning. The tyre was then nailed on with tyre nails. These tyres would have to be periodically renewed, and on some carriages summer and winter tyres would be alternated.

Sadly Rodney closed his forge in 1988 to end a long tradition of three generations of his family; now only Andy Powell remains to keep up a long tradition of forges in Wadhurst - as well as being a pillar of the local fire brigade.

Bassett's forge - in 1930

WADHURST PARK IN VICTORIA'S REIGN

MARIT RAUSING

Wadhurst Park stands on the Wealden Heights, 400 feet up, in East Sussex, close to the Sussex - Kent border. It was originally called High Town, probably until 1870 when the Spanish Murrieta family bought the property.

Wadhurst Park has been inhabited since the Middle Ages. It is first mentioned in a subsidy roll of 1295 (doubtless to raise money for Edward I's wars against the Scots). In 1483 it is recorded as the home of Sir Robert Maunser, a substantial landowner, whose descendants were great iron masters. They married into other important families in the neighbourhood; the Barhams, the Newingtons and the Bakers.

The Maunser family built several houses on the site. A map from 1652 shows an Elizabethan manor house, half-timbered and gabled, with outbuildings and a church. The estate measured 303 acres and included a hammer pond, made by damming up the stream near the present Buttons Farm. This would have been used to work the adjacent iron forges. In the stream black stones, possibly slag, are still found.

A map from 1839 shows High Town with a house, garden outbuildings and cottages, but no church. The acreage is now slightly less, 261 acres.

In 1870 the estate was sold to Cristobal and Adriano de Murrieta, two bachelor brothers of a wealthy Spanish family. Their married brother José made his residence at Wadhurst Park. The Murrieta forebears came from Santurce, near Bilbao, in the north of Spain, from where they had emigrated to South America. In the course of two generations they had amassed a great fortune by trading, especially with Argentina. Eventually they returned to Europe and settled in England, where 'C. de Murrieta and Co.' developed into a firm of great importance. Don José was given the title of Marques de Santurce in October 1877 by King Alfonso XII in recognition of the many services he had rendered Spain. His wife was also Spanish, with her origins in Santurce. It was she who undoubtedly contributed a great deal towards achieving the high position the family held in English society. She was clever and fascinating as well as beautiful and a great favourite of the late King Edward VII.

Among the frequent guests at Wadhurst Park were Lord Randolph Churchill, Billy Oliphant, Lord Charles Beresford and Arthur Balfour, who often came to relax in the pleasant atmosphere at the Murrieta's new family seat. Edward VII, as Prince of Wales, rarely seemed happier and more at ease than at Wadhurst Park.

All this lavish entertaining called for a big, comfortable house. After having bought Wadhurst Park in 1870 the family immediately engaged the English architect Edward J Tarver to build a house on the site, incorporating an existing house to serve as domestic offices. The new house had high ceilings, a tower with an adjoining gallery and no less than five W.C.s. *The Builder,* May 19, 1877, shows an engraving of the central hall of the house and gives information about the house in general. The house was built by a Mr Shearburn from Dorking and had cost to date £12,000. In *The Builder,* April 12, 1884, Mr Tarver reported about new developments at Wadhurst Park. The house had been added to, a new bigger dining room had been created, the old one being too small for "such distinguished guests as The Prince of Wales", as Mr Tarver put it. Wadhurst Hall was claimed to have been the first country house in England with several dining tables in the dining room. A long range of stables for summering hunters, new farmsteads, one called Flattenden", the other "Combe", had been built, a chapel lined with reproduction Spanish tiles had been erected and a conservatory built to make the approach to the chapel under cover.

No wonder that Wadhurst Park was called "The Princely Estate" when it was offered for sale in *The Times* ten years later. Advertised is the convenience of the South-Eastern Railway as well as the proximity to Tunbridge Wells and London. The acreage is now 1,500 and the new house is "a palatial residence". The land agents found it "impossible to convey even the most inadequate conception to the numerous beauties and advantages possessed by this charming property".

Life at Wadhurst Park was at its most splendid between the middle of the 1880's to the middle of the 1890's. A 33 acre lake was created by Irish workmen and a riding school, tennis courts, an ice rink, a tea house, a boat-house and kennels were added to all the other amenities.

Wadhurst Park became a famous shooting estate, especially known for its duck shoot. The subsequent owners kept up the duck and pheasant shoots until the Second World War. The Murrieta brothers also built what became Wadhurst College for Girls in Mayfield Lane, and Southover at Burwash Common. They also had a house in London at Carlton House Terrace where they stayed many months of the year. The brilliant entertainments given there were quite a feature of the season, and it was in that house that the weddings of José's two daughters were celebrated, with the Prince and Princess of Wales present.

The first wedding was the one of Luisa, who married Lord William Neville, the Marquess of Abergavenny's fourth son, in 1889. It took place in Brompton Oratory, both bride and groom being Catholic. The young lord had created a great flutter in society by becoming a Roman Catholic several years before he met Luisa, and his father cut him off without a penny. So he took to business, starting work in José's office. He promptly fell in love with his employer's elder daughter Luisa.

The wedding was a social event, but what was particularly commented upon was the fact that the Prince of Wales honoured the family with his presence in the Oratory. A great deal of criticism of the Prince was voiced at the time. It was said that he, as heir to the throne of a Protestant country and 'Defender of the Faith', ought not to attend a Roman Catholic service in his country. But to him mere forms of religion were not very important. The anti-Roman Catholic Coronation oath which tradition forced him to take was a great source of distress to him, and he successfully worked for its abolition.

The Prince must have felt sympathy and friendship for the young couple, for when he learnt that they had arranged to leave for Paris the same night to spend their honeymoon there, he said to them: "I hear you are off for Paris and as I am also leaving to go there tonight, will you come and travel with me in my special train and boat?". The young couple accepted the gracious invitation, but the bride never forgot how shy she felt on arriving at Calais where a special supper had been prepared for the Prince by the mayor and to which she and the bridegroom were also invited.

One and a half years later, in 1891, the younger daughter Clara married the Spanish Duke de Santona, likewise in Brompton Oratory, and was also honoured by the presence of the Prince and Princess of Wales. Their first born child, a boy, died at birth and was buried in the crypt of the chapel in Wadhurst Hall.

The brilliant years at Wadhurst Park and Carlton House Terrace found a tragic end. In 1890 the financial house of Baring was thrown into crisis when Argentina defaulted on bond payments. The Murrietas were heavily involved with the Argentine Railways and lost their fortune in the aftermath of the crisis. Both Wadhurst Park and the house in Carlton House Terrace had to be sold.

THE DREWES

In June 1898 Wadhurst Park was sold to Mr Julius C Drew (changed to Drewe in 1913), who had started his working life as a tea buyer in China. He opened his first shop in Liverpool in 1878; in 1883 he moved to London. The business developed rapidly under the name of 'The Home and Colonial Stores'. After only six years he and his partner John Musker were able to retire from active participation in the firm as rich men. Drewe was only thirty-three years old. In 1890 he bought Culverden Castle in Tunbridge Wells, on which site the Kent and Sussex Hospital now stands, and at that time married Frances Richardson. Already by 1900 he was listed as Drew of Wadhurst Hall in *Burke's Landed Gentry*.

Julius Drewe bought Wadhurst Park lock, stock and barrel. He paid £47,850 for the whole estate; it was described in the sales contract as the "Manor of Combe or Coombes and its lands, the Mansion House known as Wadhurst Hall, together with the Park, Lake, Gardens, Pleasure Grounds, Stabling and Outbuildings and the land in the Parishes of Wadhurst, Mayfield and Ticehurst, known as the Wadhurst Park Estate". Mr Drewe added new land to the estate and put in central heating and electricity from a turbine by the lake. He then moved into his new home with his young wife and three sons, Adrian, Basil and Cedric, born between 1891 and 1896. The first born was named after Adriano de Murrieta.

Two daughters, Mary and Frances, were born at Wadhurst Hall. Life there seems to have been blissfully happy. Frances has given an account of her childhood, which reads like a fairytale; the sweet, kind parents with their five children, surrounded by friendly, devoted servants in the most comfortable and beautiful setting. She mentions many of the servants by name: Mr Waite, the butler, with his marvellous mutton-chop whiskers and his wife who made dresses; Mrs Stacey, the housekeeper, busy by the sewing machine in her work room; Mrs Chandler, the cook, who was chef-trained; the much-loved nanny Bernie Rickwood, nicknamed Bop; the second nanny Mary Jane Sharpe and the nursery maid Eliza Winch, who lived with her parents in Stream Cottages by the Miners' Arms. Eliza's husband worked in the kitchen garden. Her father prepared kindling wood in the cellar of Wadhurst Hall. There were White, the estate carpenter; Barnes, the sweeper of the front drive; Hutton and later on Grant, the coachmen; Mrs Bradshaw, the head laundress, married to the previous estate carpenter. There were the two drivers, Holter and Nethercot; Mr and Mrs Dunk - Mr Dunk nursing the Drewe boys when they got the measles, Mrs Dunk cooking for the unmarried men living in the Bothy. There was Mr Crawford at Scrag Oak, the estate agent, who every Christmas handed out turkeys and geese to the people working at Wadhurst Park. There were the under-keepers, Wickens and Everett; the latter reared the ducks at Doozes Farm. There was the charming Irish governess, Miss Jennie Griffith, known as Griff, and the Chaplain Leslie Stevenson at Sunset Lodge. He later became vicar of Wadhurst, then Canon and Dean of Waterford Cathedral. In the Entrance Lodge lived the Friend family, and at the Octagon Lodge by the back drive lived the Necklins. Mr Friend and Mr Necklin both served as night-watchmen.

The main drive was flanked by glaucous cedars planted by the Murrietas. The Hall, still with the Spanish furniture, smelled of bees' wax polish. The floors were covered by carpets from Donegal which Mr Drewe had ordered when he bought the house. Morning prayers with all the staff were held in the dining-room. The family had many clergymen among their friends, Mr Drewe being the son of an evangelical clergyman himself. Sunday service was always in the Chapel; Mr Drewe taught Sunday-school to the senior boys, his daughter Mary to the smaller children. Elaborate Christmas tree parties were held in the riding school for all the people working on the estate, with heaps of presents and a huge tea to follow. In the summer there were garden parties with pastoral plays and tea in marquees. There were shooting parties every Saturday during the season with enormous bags of ducks and pheasants, followed by tea in the hall, alternating with dinner parties with the children kneeling in the gallery to catch a glimpse of their beautiful mother going in to dinner. Occasionally balls took place in the huge Oak Room, where the orchestra sat comfortably playing in the ingle-nook. In the summer, lunches were served on the terrace with screens to keep out the draught and light shades to keep out the sun.

Julius Drewe did a great deal of charitable work. He started a Clubroom in what is now Mayhurst, and a book club for young unmarried men. He also supported for many years a Dr Packard, who was a medical man and a clergyman as well, who had his surgery in Shoreditch in the East End of London.

133

All the Drewe children played musical instruments, and their mother played the piano. Every Sunday evening the family sang hymns together. There was plenty of sport. Wadhurst Park had its own cricket and football teams. There were both lawn tennis and ordinary tennis, croquet, ice-skating in the winter, roller-skating in the riding school and riding. The children had their own ponies, a donkey, a monkey and many other pets. There were the kennels with spaniels, setters, pointers and retrievers; there was fishing in the lake and Saturday afternoon shooting with father.

The gardens were a source of joy, fruit and flower gardens beyond the conservatory, vegetable gardens by Sunset Lodge and a marvellous rose garden beneath the terraces. The rose garden was Mrs Drewe's favourite place. The children were sent to choose roses for the male guests, to wear in their button holes for dinner, and during summer the kind Mrs Drewe used to send baskets of roses to her sons at Eton.

Mr Drewe liked modern comforts. Wadhurst Hall had central heating, electricity, an estate telephone and several cars among them two Rolls Royces with fur-lined rugs and foot-warmers.

The Drewes were a close-knit family. House guests were mainly relatives, clergymen and business acquaintances. But business was never mentioned. Mr Drewe had amassed a great fortune, and he was satisfied that he had done so in an honest way.

Daily life was comfortable and leisurely. Both Mr and Mrs Drewe were slow eaters and the meals were lengthy with handwritten menus. Nothing was left to chance. Mrs Drewe always inspected the guest-rooms herself before visitors arrived. Mr Drewe attended to estate matters in the morning, using the telephone in his dressing room. He read his evening newspaper, fetched for him at the railway station by a boy with a pony and trap. He went for walks, fished in the lake, did some shooting and went to Scotland, and later to Torquay, for his holidays.

A complementary account of life at Wadhurst Park has been given by Mr Leonard Pierce, the secretary of Goudhurst and Kilndown Local History Society. Mr Pierce's father came to Wadhurst Hall as a single gardener, married and was given a cottage on the estate, where a daughter and two sons were born. Like Frances Drewe, Leonard Pierce remembers his childhood as a golden age, where Wadhurst Hall was the centre of the universe and Mr Drewe its benevolent master. Some of the people mentioned by Frances Drewe were also important to him. Old Granny Necklin in the Octagon Lodge and the Friend family in the Entrance Lodge; Mr Dunk, who not only looked after the Drewe boys when they were ill but was also in charge of hundreds of hens. The Dunks lived in a cottage called Glenhurst attached to the Clubroom (Mayhurst).

The cricket field and football pitch were on either side of Button's Drive and, after matches, the teams resorted to the Clubroom in Mayhurst, with its entrance maxim 'Manners Makyth Man'. Wadhurst Hall had not only a football team, it also had its own football song, composed by one of the keepers.

On the ball Wadhurst Hall
Never mind the danger
Rush it in and score a goal
Play just like a ranger.
Mark your man and tackle fair
Keep well on the ball
A jolly lot of lads are they
Who play for Wadhurst Hall.

From the Working Album of Nathaniel Hitch - sculptor: design for the chimneypiece in the Great Hall of Wadhurst Hall [photo from the Henry Moore Institute Archive, Liverpool]. The History Society was recently asked for help in explaining the connection with the de Murrieta family.

During the 1914-18 war Wadhurst Hall had its own squad of uniformed volunteers, jocularly known as 'The Nanny Goat Lancers'. The Pierce children went to school in Tidebrook, a two-mile walk from Wadhurst Hall. They were joined on their way to school by Mary Maylam, whose parents farmed Lodge Hill, together with their two sons. The children often went to the laundry along the road to the kennels. The laundry was warm and inviting in cold weather. Three or four girls worked there, washing and ironing for the Hall. When the Drewes went to Torquay in the summer, the laundry maids went with them. During the absence of the Drewes the lake was there for the children on the estate to explore. A barge moored by the boat-house was ideal as a bathing platform. At the end of the lake was the Tea House, a wooden chalet type of building, where lunches were served during the shoots. Mr Darkins, the head keeper, allotted each guest a boy who carried his cartridge bag for the day. The beating was done by the men on the estate. The game was hung in the game larder, a louvered building near the kennels. It still stands within the freehold of the Hunting Lodge (known earlier as Maywood

135

and before that Rose Cottage). During the Murrieta time an ice house in a bank near the Hall was used.

Christmas was a great time enjoyed by all with Christmas dinner provided by Mr Drewe. On Boxing Day the Wadhurst Town Band came to play carols, first at the front door for the gentry and then at the back door for the staff. Then came the great party in the riding school, described also by Miss Frances. The family and the staff rendered songs and recitations.

After leaving school, Leonard Pierce was taken on as a garden boy. He then lived with his parents in Chevincote, now held freehold for more than 40 years by Mr and Mrs Winchester. Around the cottage was the fruit garden. In front of the house across the road were the pleasure grounds, flower borders with box hedges, long glass houses and the great conservatory with palms and ferns.

On the other side of the conservatory was the terrace, covered with fine beach pebbles that needed constant raking to keep it looking nice. Sheep were on loan from the house farm (Flattenden) to keep the grass down by the drive near the house and Leonard was there to herd them off the borders round the drive.

At the annual ball he was employed to guide the chauffeurs to the garage yard, when they had deposited their charges at the front door.

His most important job, though, was in the Chapel, where he rang the chapel bell for service every Sunday. His mother played the organ and he acted as a verger, getting the key early on Sunday morning from the key rack in the butler's pantry. Once a quarter he presented himself at the estate agents with an account which read: "Due to Leonard Pierce for church work, Thirteen Shillings".

He was christened by the aforementioned Dr Packard from Shoreditch and instructed for confirmation by Mr Turnbill, who came up from Bexhill for the weekends staying at Sunset Lodge, where Mr Waite, the butler, now lived. Sunset Lodge later became the property of Sir Willis Combs. Mr Pierce snr then took a job as head gardener in Tunbridge Wells, and so young Leonard's carefree, happy life at Wadhurst Hall came to an abrupt end!

The Drewe's eldest son Adrian died during the First World War. He served in the army like his two younger brothers. His death was a terrible loss and Mr Drewe never fully recovered from the shock. He had by then already lost interest in Wadhurst Park, a place bought ready-made and although beautiful and agreeable not in any sense his creation. Early on he had left his business in the hands of others and in 1919 he and his partner sold the outstanding shares for £1 million, a huge sum in those days.

With his elder brother William he had always taken a keen interest in the history of the Drewe family. A genealogist convinced him that his family was descended from the Drewes of Broadhembury near Honiton in Devon. Already in 1901 he bought land there and installed his brother William, a barrister of the Inner Temple, at Broadhembury House. Their first cousin Richard Peek was the rector of Drewsteighton, named after Drogo de Teigne, and alleged forefather to the Drewes. Julius stayed on several occasions with his cousin and it must have been here that he conceived the idea of building a castle on the home ground of his ancestor. He found an ideal site, and in 1910 he bought about 450 acres south and west of the village. (By the time of his death in 1931 he had bought up an estate of 1,500 acres). He then went to Edwin Lutyens, the most interesting architect of the time, and asked him to build his castle. According to his son Basil, he did so on the advice of William Hudson, proprietor of *Country Life,* who was both a patron and a champion of Lutyens.

Drewe was now 54 years old, but he still had time and energy and money to create his new family seat. On April 4, 1911, a foundation stone was laid. Castle Drogo was finally completed in 1930, a year before Drewe died. In 1927 the furniture, mainly the Murrieta's Spanish pieces, was brought down from Wadhurst Hall.

Mrs Drewe and her son Basil continued to live at Castle Drogo. During 1939-45, Mrs Drewe and her daughter Mary ran the house as a home for babies made homeless during the bombings of London.

Mrs Drewe died in 1954 and Basil Drewe was then joined at Drogo by his son Anthony and his wife. Anthony and his son, Dr Christopher Drewe, later gave Castle Drogo and 600 acres of the surrounding land to the National Trust.

INDEX

The index is in three parts - first a subject index, showing the start pages for the item or the page on which the subject is discussed. Then there is an index of places named in the articles. Next, there is an index of people mentioned in the texts: where more than one member of a family appears on the same page, only one entry has been indexed. Finally, the illustrations are indexed.

SUBJECT INDEX

LOCATION INDEX

NAMES INDEX

INDEX OF ILLUSTRATIONS

Set as a pdf file in Perpetua 12pt and published by Greenman Enterprise

Greenman Farm, Wadhurst, Sussex TN5 6LE

and printed and bound by The Ink Pot

Southbank House, Victoria Road, Southborough, Kent, TN4 0LT

ISBN 0-9545802-1-4